Akin Olagunju

Warship

Akin Olagunju

Warship

Beliefs and Superstitions

JustFiction Edition

Publisher:
JustFiction! Edition
is a trademark of
International Book Market Service Ltd., member of OmniScriptum Publishing Group
17 Meldrum Street, Beau Bassin 71504, Mauritius
Printed at: see last page
ISBN: 978-620-0-49165-7

Akin Olagunju

Warship

<u>**Dedication**</u>

I dedicate this book to God Almighty and everyone who has shown me love directly or indirectly.

And also to Chleo and Ceaser, our 2 loving adult dogs that died mysteriously within a space of a week, we miss you.

Chapter One

A gospel worship song is heard playing in the background, its being played by Ireti (Tunde's wife), she was singing along as Tunde pulls over the parking lot. The song continues to play at the background as Tunde arranges himself from his car (Honda Accord EOD) to the living room. Afterwards, Ireti notices his presence and prays that God give the family everything they want especially the area of their financial life.

Tunde thereafter carries his 2 year old daughter (Daisy) and the song fades away.

(one week later....)

Tunde's phone ringing *"Hon. Jerry calling"*

Hon – Jerry – the money has dropped.. yes... I just got the alert .. come to my office right now, im going out soon..

Tunde – alright ... im on my way

(Hon. Jerry's office..)

Tunde – that client is sure o.. see how he paid on time. Bad clients will make you feel like there are no good clients out there. Just imagine how this guy paid "sharp sharp"

Hon. Jerry – Mr. Tunde, God works in mysterious ways .. see this Job, small job that we did, this guy released 10,000,000

hmm..see.... I'm a man of my word, **five million naira** is yours. I told you we will split 50/50

Tunde – See ehn.. this is a secret... let your wife be praying for you o... since my woman prayed for me last week... I have been meeting nice people.. I met you just recently ..now you are willing to give me 5,000,000 because you said so .. isn't that just great?

Camera shows time to tell 4:30pm ... camera shows Tunde's disappointed face as he said

Tunde – "bank" (quietly)

Tunde's House

As Tunde steps into his house .. with the bag.

he didn't stop to greet anyone at the living room .. heads straight to his bedroom.

He hides the money away and relaxes completely well in the room.. Ireti comes in few moments later ..... told him about his favorite meal fixed at the dining

Tunde insists he will like to have his dinner in the room.

Ireti – (makes jest) you are the one who complains not to eat anywhere else but the dining .. anyways.. I'm coming.

(She comes in with the food .. finished eating..)

Tunde – I have a secret for you (whispers) Babe that job paid off.. now I have money.. (whispers more faintly) Five million Naira..

Ireti shows excitement as Scene fades off.

(An analog wall clock tells 9:15pm as time while digital time displays on screen)

Then 10 pm shows the couple about to sleep .. then 12am ... wife sleeping .. Tunde finds it hard to sleep by turning on the bed... then 1:15am .. Tunde goes into the guest's room closing and arranging the curtains making sure that nobody can see from outside... then 1:30am Tunde is seen counting the money and some cash well arranged on the bed ... he starts writing some details on a jotter calculating ... the answer of his calculation is seen when he wrote on his jotter = 5,000,000 ...satisfied with his calculating skills, he arranged the money back in the bag.. 2:15am putting the money back to where he initially kept it 2:20am he switches off his light and sleeps off..

7:45am

He puts the money at the back seat of his Honda, he covered the bag with his old suit rack and started off towards the bank. He was putting on corporate with his shirt well tucked in. A transparent glasses on his face. Well alive.

At the traffic junction just before the bank, he stopped and wound down his car window to buy a bottle of water, a well dressed youngman met up with him and says,

Young Man - "please I uhhmm.. I came to this area and the guy I came to see is not home, I'm kinda stranded.. I will appreciate anything you give me... I.. really need your help

Tunde's face reacts as if he's about to oblige the young man.. rather he slowly turns to the water vendor ... got a bottle.. collects his change .... Faces his front ... winds up his window.. opens the bottle .. enjoyed few gulps of water Light turns green.. he zoomed off blatantly ignoring the guy.

He got to the bank and asked where the Manager's office is.. he was shown the way and he entered the office with the bag of money.

(he saw an average height dark man)

Tunde - My manager! Any other Manager is a counterfeit!

Bank Manager – Goodmorning Sir you're welcome... im not sure ive seen this face..

(Tunde interjects)

Tunde – No ..no.. no... we haven't met before you see.. im one of your bank's esteemed customers .... amongst the banks I bank with .. i like your modus operandi and u seem to have reliable securities too.. (looks around and whispers... I want to deposit 5,000,000..) ... uhmmm... im sure you people will have a party after im gone cuz this must be the ... never mind .... I have one question... is my money safe here??

Bank Manager – Mr. Tunde .. we don't only double the profit of our customers deposits .. we make sure we give our customers peace of mind and also the value for their money.

Tunde – don't worry say no more... Please let me have your personal phone number .. so we can be talking often.

(a lady staff comes in with a cup of coffee for Tunde)

Bank Manager – ha... no problem at all, you can call me anytime for any enquiries. 0803926..

Tunde – take this money ..(hands him the money) please deposit it in my account.

Bank Manager – No problem Sir.. we are at your service.

Tunde leaves the office and went to work

(at the gate of his office Tunde's phone beeps.. he checks it) it reads

Account Balance – **5,220,000** (digital on screen as he checks his phone)

(Tunde's workplace)

(during an office meeting)

Work Manager : I am happy to be present here with you at our quarterly meeting .. I hope by the end of today's deliberation we will be able to strike off all the important agenda off our list

As you can see, we are making tremendous progress in all our Contracts... though we are yet to be paid , if not we will all be sharing profits by now.. So for now, just manage your salaries ... anyways.... These contracts are not 100% completed yet, we all need to be patient...

Any other business?

Staff One : Ermm... Yes Sir, you said something about our upward salary review at the last meeting.. im surprised our salary is still pegged... has the management changed their mind?

Tunde: I thought no one would ask *(subtly)*

(the whole staff seems excited about the question and turns to the manager in anticipation of the answer)

Work Manager : well the management has not changed its mind.. we have the interest of the staff of this company at heart... its just that due to the prevailing economic situation... the Company has not charted a way everybody's salary would be reviewed and paid without affecting the assets of the company...

(Camera shows reaction of staff reluctantly agreeing to the explanation)

Tunde : (stutters a bit) but S ssir.. what about the fleet of cars just acquired by the company for the board of directors and summer vacations enjoyed by their family? I wasn't going to mention that... but since you said something about the prevailing economic situation ... I feel in the interest of fairness and everyone here present for the person presiding over this meeting .. the person of your esteemed self to explain to us...

(someone mistakingly claps her hands but calms down when She drew attention)

Work Manager - well im almost flattered by the closing remark of your question.. you need to understand this is a public company, our shares and clientele are growing because of the way we treat our Staff...

(Someone coughs)

Work Manager: (gets distracted.... continues) but y'know we need to give our subscribers a show, a show of luxury, to let them know we are not doing bad as a company

Tunde: but the directors are the celebrities.. isn't it? the welfare of a working staff is more important ..with all due respect

Work Manager: we all have to put in extra effort to come up in life to enjoy these privileges (stares at Tunde Sternly)... there is no father Christmas anywhere ... I'm tired of all of these.... Any other business?

Female Staff : I'm happy to inform you that Ifeoma in accounting department is getting married next month 16ᵗʰ to be precise..

(All cheers) (Ifeoma stands up)

Work Manager: that's a great one, we like to celebrate ourselves and as our custom and tradition .. we all know what is expected of us ..

Female Staff : we have a schedule of the people who have indicated interest to attend the wedding, its at Imo state.. and we also have a table of how everyone sitting here is to contribute to support Ifeoma ...

(the amount is boldy written at the back of the invitation card..Shares invitation cards to everyone)

Tunde: (scoffs) you people came ready.. theres no father Christmas anywhere

(Scene fades off)

(Following day at the bank...Knocks the door twice .. didn't wait for response enters the Manager's office)

Tunde – Mr. Managerial Duties.. (in a lively mood)

Bank Manager – Ha... our esteemed Customer Mr. Tunde Ajisafe .. you are most welcome.. just yesterday you were here to deposit 5m .. a little secret? That was why you got a complimentary Cup of coffee yesterday .. you remember ? that coffee .. the one my secretary fixed you? Nevermind.. I probably shouldn't have mentioned that.. Im sure as we have seen you today, you are here deposit another amount? Or No? im saying too much ... How may I help you?

Tunde – heeeen .... Not at all .. you know .. you cant pass in front of the palace and not greet the king.. (laughs) that's on a lighter note.. im on my way to work.. so I thought I should drop by and see you and probably ask you if that 5m I deposited yesterday is still there?

Bank Manager – Haba Mr. Tunde.. our Customers money are always safe with us, we have we have our securities at NDIC that insures our customer's money.. and around the bank we have 4 police officers with ak 47.. we are well protected

Tunde – so my money is safe ehn?

Bank Manager – Very safe... anytime you need your 5m .. you can withdraw it

Tunde – the particular notes I deposited?

Bank Manager - What?

Tunde – I was just kidding ... that money legit.. I made it clean .. so you know I kinda love that cash.

Bank Manager- it cant be that particular one you deposited now.. I mean...we will make sure your 5m is complete anytime you need it

Tunde – So its not the particular cash I deposited I will get?

Bank Manager – I may not be sure about any other thing like .. which country smokes indian hemp most .. but im sure about this one.. its not that particular cash...

Tunde - well.. have a nice day.. im off to work

(as Tunde took off.. he looks more paranoid)

Tunde enters a filling station to buy fuel... 3 cars are before him

A red car got his attention .. by the red car is a boy in his twenties wearing a yellow top. The red car is like 15 meters away.. Tunde suspects the red car must have bought his own fuel and about to leave the filling station before accosted by the boy.

Tunde did not hear what they were saying because they were far apart but he saw that the driver gave the boy some money.

Tunde was moving slowly to the pump

 By this time.. it was Tunde's turn to buy fuel

Tunde -Please Put 5k ...

After the vendor finished dispensing the fuel, he drove to buy snacks by the supermarket. He stopped his engine from running, got out of his car and got to where the snacks were showcased

Vendor – what do you care for Sir?

Tunde – meatpie and soft drinks

Vendor- Ok (vendors hands Tunde the beverages) your money is N500

Tunde gives the Vendor N1000 note expecting his change.

Boy – Uhmm ... Please Excccusee me sir?

Tunde turns and saw the boy with the yellow top with the red car... anger was written all over his face.. he knew he was about to be begged for money .. he managed to compose himself and asks...

Tunde – Yyes?

Boy – Sir ... sorry to bother you Sir, I am a student .. I was posted to **Tazzrev** bank for my internship... unfortunately Sir, I was rejected...

Tunde – and so? How's is that my business? Do I look like I work at Tazzrev bank?

Boy – No Sir... I need to go back to my school to be reposted to another place.. I don't have enough money for my transport

Tunde – Mtscheeeww.. (Turns to Vendor) my friend... where is my change? I don't have all day... if not for you.. will this jobless scammer meet me here?

Vendor – Sorry Sir.. we don't have 500 change... we have only 400... but if you have N100 I will give you N600 I have 3 pieces of 200 notes

Tunde – I don't have 100, give me 400 (turns to the boy) you are still here? My friend get lost! (Boy leaves by an inch .. he didn't really move)

Tunde notices a sad face on the Vendor's face pitying the boy.

Tunde – you know what? Hey! look here.. (turns to Vendor) give this boy a bottle of water with my 100 Change... (faces the boy..) I have you people's time today.

Vendor- (hands the boy a bottle of water but not happy because she thought the 100 was hers)

Tunde – see my friend .. you cant tell me you are not a scammer... you are well dressed ... and I initially saw you taxing a red car. Ohh... you didn't know ... everyday is for the thief.. one day for the owner... I could get you arrested you know?

Boy- Sir ... it hasn't gotten to that .. I was explaining my predicament to the woman but she only gave me 100 .. my transport fare is 500.

Tunde – oh really? Ok ... whats the name of your school?

Boy – New Horizon state university

Tunde- what are you studying?

Boy – Psychology

Tunde – Psychology? You must think im stupid.. how can a psychology student be posted to a bank for internship?

Boy – that was the same question the bank manager asked ... the reason I was rejected.

Tunde – hmmm ... that makes sense .. oh you saw the manager of Tazzrev bank?

Boy- Yes Sir... I even told him I didn't have money for transport .. he didn't give me anything, he said its not his business

Tunde – the manager is a fat fair man? (testing him)

Boy – No Sir, a skinny black man

Tunde – hmmm... let me see your posting letter

(boy hands Tunde the letter)

Tunde- (Convinced) but then .. you cant blame random people for your problems.. we all have problems.. im not your god, neither am I government... Its bad to beg.. If I were you .. I will look for a little hustle to do.. to make sure my transport fare is complete... in the alternative .. trek to the school... im sorry my friend I cant help you (Tunde's phone beeps) see ive wasted all my time here, ive got to go... use the water I bought you to keep yourself hydrated as you trek to wherever you are going.. See my friend, Reflect on everything ive told you and tell yourself ... its bad to beg.. there is no father Christmas anywhere....

(Tunde zooms off)

Boy: (standstill)

(Tunde reverses his car ...)

Tunde - Whats your name?

Boy: Timothy

Tunde: Timo..??

Boy: (interjects) but you can call me Tim

Tunde: Tim? (laughs) you are something else.. can you use a computer?

Boy: very well Sir... But Im not doing yahoo *"internet fraud"* O (raises up his hands)

Tunde : what? Hope u are not a criminal (points finger at him?)

Boy: Haba .. No sir not at all that's why im askin.. rather beggin' .. you..

Tunde: don't say the word begging... its bad ..people do it everytime.. even on social media.. look ! you are complete... and u are not disabled well... Give me your number ... I may have a use for you ... at least.. "na student u be" ... a great future lies ahead of you.

(gives Tunde his number and returns Tunde's phone)

Boy – thank you sir.. I will make you proud sir.. (Tunde gives him a funny look and takes his leave......as Tunde was about to leave .. the Boy expects him to give money)

Tunde – I already made myself clear .. No money... start trekking... as you are trekking, use that time to think about your life.. there are two types of people in this life .. the ones who give and those who beg.. ask yourself...

Timothy – (Tim turns and started going) goodbye Sir

(Tunde leaves, takes first turn and completely disappeared from the road)

(Tunde's office.. only Tunde and Jess occupies this office.. a neatly arranged office "themed white")

Jess – Jessica is seen touching up herself using her portable mirror.. Tunde in the background) " I wonder why I even came to the office today.. I have a doctor's appointment by 12

Tunde – well u came because you have to earn the money to pay the Doctor

Jess – Excuseee Me! .. I have a husband ... and my parents are still very much around (rolling her eyes) .. the money I earn is for me alone .. I am their responsibility .. they have to take care of me as an omalicha that I am (smiles as she looks at the mirror... Tunde also looking at her funny .. smiling)

(A female staff enters their office)

Office staff – Goodmorning mr Tunde

Tunde – what can I do for you this morning.. Toyosi? (smiling)

Toyosi – Yyes Sir.. Ifeoma's wedding is next week … we intend to send our contributions to her account tomorrow Friday

Tunde – Oh that's right.. but uhhmmm… I don't think I will attend .. I have some things I will be doing at that time

Toyosi – ehn doesn't matter Sir.. its just to support her .. you know wish her well.. even if you are not going … Aunty Jess (gestures at Jess) is not going .. but she already paid her own N20k

Jess – Please …im a big girl (faces front and feeling proud)

Tunde – Twenty what? How much did you people put.. (he rushes to bring out the invitation card from his drawers … checks the back and sees 20k … checks his name … "cordially invites Mr and Mrs Tunde Ajisafe" (shouting) Twenty thousand? Am I the one that say she should go and marry? How much is my salar.. you know what? Toyosi (talking to Office staff) .. how much did you contribute?

Toyosi – 10k

Tunde – so why are we paying 20K?

Toyosi – because Sir.. u see this your office .. is the bridge between the senior and the junior staff.. that's why?

Tunde – (looks at her in disbelief) you even have an explanation…how much are you benefitting from this transaction? Is she paying you?

Toyosi – (hisses) Mtsheew.. if you don't want to give just say it.. I wont stand here while you insult me… Exxxcccusssee me! (she heads towards the door)

Tunde – Toyosi … im sorry … it just that .. the money is a lot .. I have a family too..and.. I don't even know that ifeoma like that …which ifeoma self?

Toyosi – the one in Accounting … we have only one Ifeoma in this company Mr. Tunde

Tunde – see.. let me check my account balance .. maybe I can squeeze out 10k .. because … shey you were present at the meeting? … the prevailing economic…

(Tunde and Toyosi choruses "situation")

Tunde - .. and there is no father Christmas anywhere

Tunde – (checks account balance) – balance reads **5,210,000**… (balance displays on screen) let me transfer 10k to you right now.. that's all I can afford to part with right now…whats your account number ?

Toyosi – (receives 10k alert) you have really tried sir (rolls her eyes)

Tunde – I mean.. it's always a privilege to give back to the society…

(Toyosi leaves office… Tunde's phone beeps… receives debit alert – balance reads **5,209,900**)

Tunde – Chai! 100 naira bank charges ??? whats going on in this country.. ehn Jess?

Jess – Please o .. Mr Tunde .. don't infect me with your Aka gum "means stingy disease" …don't ask me questions…. Infact let me go and see my Doctor now…because Aka gum is a very contagious disease (standing up and heading towards the door)

Tunde – hurr… I blame you? … coming from someone that wont pay her own medical bills

Jess – ehn? Mr. Tunde … so you are using that against me? Its our family doctor! Asides that… Let me tell you the something …(alert enters) ive got people that love me… I have a good heart and im extremely beautiful … unlike you … nobody… infact… there is no need .. I reserve my comment … mtsheeeew (finishes Tunde with her eyes as she leaves the office)

Tunde – which work do you do anyways.. I do all the work around here.

Chapter Two

(Tunde's house)

Ireti – heey babe .. hows my baby boy doing?

Tunde – work was Niccccceeee .. Tomorrow is Friday ... I cant wait for the weekend baby ... how's Daisy?

Ireti – shes fine.. she has little Temperature though .. im sure she'll be fine

Tunde – alright .. hope she has eaten?

Ireti– yeesss.. she had small noodles... she's okay (raises voice a bit)

Tunde – alright (switches channel by pointing remote)

(another interval same night... Tunde almost dozing off)

Ireti – Food's ready

Tunde – okay ... (stands up and faces dining)

(Next Morning .. Friday)

(Tunde wearing his wristwatch... and cufflinks)

Ireti – Daisy temperature still high... I might need to take her to the hospital

Tunde – Hospital ? is it that serious?

Ireti – I guueesss so

Tunde – Nawa o.. me I don't like that Hospital idea (as he walks towards Daisy and put his hand on her head to check her temperature) Haha.. this is not waaaay overboard.. did u give her drugs yesterday?

Ireti – No .. just fruits

Tunde – Oo that's fine .. get her paracetamol, vitamin c and maybe blood tonic.. she will be fine she'll just sleep it off

Ireti – No.. I will take her to the hospital

Tunde – why do you want to take her to the hospital?

Ireti – because she needs medical attent... didn't you feel her temperature...? Wait .. Tunde we as a family .. we have passed this level (gesticulates) when did you become a doctor or pharmacist? ... (mimicks Tunde) get her paracetamol .. paracetamol ko – choroquine ni..

(Comes closer to Tunde)

Ireti - What im saying is.. we are millionaires now ..

Tunde – So this is what its about? Because we are Millionaires .. I should give Doctors my money..

Ireti – No no.. not that .. its not even about you paying .. I will pay if situation warrants.. I mean... we are above this standards (Daisy starts crying)

Tunde – see what you have caused now? (facing Daisy ... carries her up) Making me look like the bad guy, like a father who doesn't...forget that... See what I have in the bank now is 5m (digital show of Tunde's account balance to read 5,209,900) .. u know .. five million is a round figure .. it shouldn't go below that... I wan' hustle more (gesticulates) and make it ten million .. that's how you live life.. you need to have have savings ... you don't up your standards? (scoffs) up your standards ...for who?

Ireti – Ok ive heard .. give me my daughter..(collect and carries Daisy from Tunde) give me money for the paracetamol..

Tunde – I thought you said you will take her to the hospital?

Ireti – Oh now .. you want me to take her to the hospital?

Tunde – .. ehn.. as I carried her now.. her temperature is bit high .. besides aren't you not paying for it ?

(Wife looks at Tunde in disbelief)

Ireti – have a nice day at work and please come back early (enters room with Daisy)

(Tunde picking up his bag)

Tunde – don't worry I will send you something.. (turns his back) and please take her to a "normal hospital"

(Tunde pressing his phone... alert enters Wife's account)

Ireti – (Picks up phone .. gets alert of 10,000) ha ... at least .. (her balance reads – **192,000)** displays on screen

(Tunde reverses his car from compound...

...Pulls up in banks parking lot)

(camera shows smoke from a neatly tied indian hemp with "one love" by Bob Marley playing in the background... camera shows settings to reveal location to be a toilet... Tazzrev Bank Manager's Toilet)

Bank Manager - (sings along) "lets get together and feeeeel alright..." (knocks on the door)

Tunde – (Knocks the door.. outside bank Manager's office) Manager ... Manager !!

Bank Manager – a minute please!! ... you can come in.. make yourself comfortable

(Tunde enters and sits down).... (Manager stops playing music on phone... kills marijuana fire ... puts eye drops in eyes.. washes hands with soap... looks mirror again.. open tap water into mouth... rinses mouth and spits out water... puts perfume on body)

Bank Manager - Ha... Mr. Ajisafe (extremely excited and jumpy) ... how are you doing this morning? (sits on his chair)

Tunde – My managerial duties .. im okay o... it's like you are burning papers in your bathroom?

Bank Manager– (awkward silence.. looking at Tunde sternly) uhmm ... yes... some confidential papers belonging to the bank ... we have to burn them .. so a third eye doesn't see..

Tunde – ha .. han.. is that not why they invented a shredder? I mean paper shredder .. so you don't have to burn them...

Bank Manager - (startled) see .. Mr. Tunde .. its better to burn (desperate to drop the subject) seeing you today .. Friday morning .. I assume you are here for business?

Tunde – oh yes ... I have a question... uhhmm.. why do you people debit a whole 100 from my account anytime i transfer?

Bank Manager – (long pause) are you serious?

Tunde – Yes ... im serious .. as a banker .. you should know better .. that every unit of money counts ... how will you deduct a hundred units of my money from my account because I made a transfer?

Bank Manager – Sir.. if not for the fact that you are one of our high earned customers.. I would have asked customer service to attend to you.. but since you are already here ....(long silence) please any question on this subject, meet our customer service.. they are always at your service...(smiles)

Tunde – (couldn't believe his ears) well.. that's on a lighter note.. the second reason im here is to confirm if my 5,000,000 is still in your vaults

Bank Manager– (laughs) I knew you were getting to that .. yes yes … its here .. its always safe here .. your money is always safe with us (smiles)… however, Mr Tunde .. you don't need to always come here to ask after your money..

Tunde – ha han… is it not my money…?

Bank Manager – let me explain… people turn in a lot of money in our bank daily.. especially this branch … (remembers something) oh … hold on .. (picks up intercom… talks on phone) "tell Moses to come here immediately.."

(Moses enters office)

Bank Manager – Moses .. how much did you turn in yesterday ? huh?

Moses – (smiles lightly) just 15million

Tunde – wow

Bank Manager – (stands up)   you see Mr. Tunde … Moses is our most trustworthy marketer.. just yesterday he made one of our customer pay 15m .. that customer is not here today to ask if his 15m is still here … if im to ask Moses here how much he has turned in this month alone… Moses …how much have you…?

Moses – approximately 45m (feeling proud)

Tunde – see Mr. Manager… I am not here to know what your staff can or cannot do.. all I want to know is if my 5m is intact .. and you have already answered .. I am not here for any drama.. I see you as a friendly person .. and I like you .. reason I come here every once in a while to check on my money.. its ok..

The third reason…

Bank Manager - the third? (looks at Tunde unbelievably)

Tunde – yes the third reason I am here , I met one boy… Timothy … an intern posted here from New Horizon state University…

Bank Manager – (face brightens up) yes yes … he was here day before yesterday… please tell me you know him…

Tunde – uhmmm... I don't really know him.. but I met him ...

Bank Manager – please .. I regretted turning him back .. I need him , he could help me out with some small works around here .. his presentation was bad though.. but I will give him a second chance ..

Tunde – oh great .. I think he deserves a chance ... here's his number

Bank Manager – Thank you Mr Tunde.. oh... you see how God works? (realizes Moses is still there) Moses please you can go back to your duty post

Tunde – well ... thanks for having me "Managerial duties!" I need to get to work now .. its already 11:30am ... have a nice weekend

Bank Manager – Thank you Mr. Tunde .. don't forget to see the Customer service on your way out...

Tunde – Haba! Because of 100? Nooo ... im already late for work (closes door)

Bank Manager – (dials number) – Yes Timothy ... good ... good.. I want you to come right now to Tazzrev bank before 2pm ... can you make it? ... great.. I will be expecting you

Chapter Three

(Tunde's office)

Work Manager – (on intercom) Please call me Tunde

Toyosi – (enters Tunde's office) sir ... Manager is calling you sir..

(Tunde enters Manager's office)

Work Manager – how do you do today?

Tunde – Im fine Sir.. you?

Work Manager – Oh well (spreading hands) ... very well ... you can see im doing good.. we gastu work to put food on the table you know?

Tunde – (laughs) no doubt Sir

Work Manager – Tunde .. why didn't you remind me last week about the company's site? You want the contractor to swindle us? Ehn?

Tunde – Im sorry Sir .. I have a lot on my hands... that's why...

Work Manager – my friend .. sorry for yourself..

Tunde – (frowns and later smiles) but...t we can still go today sir..

Work Manager – ok ... what says your time ?

Tunde – its past 12 sir..

Work Manager – Ok .. we can still go then

(In work Manager's car)

(Manager is driving.. Tunde on passenger sit... as they were going... they got to a hold up at a junction)

Stranger – Exxccuse me Sir.. Sir .. im going to Maraba .. please help me..

(Manager carefully pulls over and allows the stranger at his back sit)

Tunde – (shows discomfort ....keeps quite the entire trip.. allows manager's car music playlist take control......)

(as soon as Manager drops off the passenger...)

Tunde – .... so that's how you used to pick up strangers?

Work Manager – yes ...(sarcastic) I do my own part...

Tunde – hmm.. Oga "means boss" ... this life .. one has to be careful... how can you just pick up a stranger ? someone you don't know .. under the guise of helping humanity.. (smiles inaudibly) you are not a god .. neither are you the government..

Work Manager – haha.. so whatever happens to "helping your neighbor"

Tunde ‑ your neighbor ? seriously? You of all people quoting a bible verse?

Work Manager – what? (frantic.. apparently manager is a die hard believer) What do you mean? See .. anytime you are in that position to help someone .. just do it .. don't think about it .. do it ... though you have to be careful .. you have to use your head but.. do it ..Let me tell you something ... Im aready 64.. next year June.. I will be 65.. I've achieved most things my seniors I used to look up to cannot even boast of, my 4 kids are all educated.. my last born graduated last year .. he is a medical doctor.. already working in London.. Im a fulfilled man. One thing has not changed since my youthful days till now.... I always give ... the more I give.. the more that is added to me .. I don't know how... I guess its just one of life mysteries.. So what? If I give a killer a lift... and he kills me and takes my car ..look.. I will die a happy man ..Not that I wish to die now.. I need to see my grandkids and all .. I need to show them how to love ..Just this morning.. My step Mom's sister called me .. told me she needed 3000 ... for something important.. I didn't question her... I just sent her 5000..Whats my own?

I mean... people have real problem...

I cant remember having any... I have nobody at the hospital, no body in jail or in court .. the only problem I can attribute to myself is the fact that people always call me everytime they need help..

But... is that a problem ?

No .. to me ... its not ... if my only problem is people calling me for help .. im happy to do it.. im happy to help .. at least its good impression..

But Tunde ... you are right ... one has to be careful

Tunde – (smiles) couldn't agree more

(Manager pulls over to the parking lot of the site... they both come out of the car)

Site worker – haaa. ... Baba Manager... hailings to your government.. na you be the main man...

Work Manager – ah... see this man .. you don start...

Site worker– Nooo ... God no go allow us offend you ooo... na you be our baba for here .... (some other site guys joins him in hailing)

Work Manager - (laughs loudly)

Site worker – see ehn.. I value you pass my life ... na because of you .. we dey wake up 4 am come site .. if no be you ... we no go send this job at all.. we wont even come! Because that your supervisor... na mumu

Work Manager – oya take .. kai ... your own too much ... ha haan .. (counts 10k and gives him)

Site worker – haaaaa!!!! This one too much ... Oga ... na up up you go dey go ... you go dey increase on every side ... chai... u burst my head today oo.. (turns his back)

Work Manager – .. come here ... No be for only you ooo ...

Site worker – haa.. baba I know .. I know...

(Tunde has been inspecting the site all along and was quite satisfied with the job done.. 25 minutes later ... comes to meet manager sitting on plastic chair of the uncompleted Plaza)

Tunde – Oga "boss".. this guys did a nice job here .. I cant even fault any of their efforts... I mean... they beat my expectation... i believe the marbles are not enough... that's why they couldn't do the finishing... but so far.. soo good ... they did an excellent job... (manager gestures in agreement) ... but sir ... don't tell them how satisfied we are with the job o (whispers...) they will not deliver well if we encourage them

Work Manager – come on.. these ones? They are loyal .. they will always give me their best, they are the ones that built my house .. have you been to my house? Yes ... they built it.. If you want the best in people.. encourage them them, have a relationship with them and let them know that you believe in them .

Tunde – Hmmm ... ok Sir

Work Manager – Suraju... oya oo.. till next week .. you know Tunde ?(pointing at Tunde) he is a quantity surveyor ... your new supervisor .. that other one is not here here again.. he messed up, he tried to scam me ..

Site worker – Ha! egbon Tunde (he raises up his hands to show loyalty... Tunde looks away)

Work Manager – he said you need more marbles .. you will get them tomorrow.. I expect this job to be done this time next week

Site worker – baba O... no lele ... next week noni.... Oya now!

(Manager and Tunde enters Car and leave)

(another day in Tunde's Office)

Jess – (making video call .. Tunde reading a spiral bound document ...)

Recipient – ehen .. baby Jessica! I love your make up o .. looking sweet as usual

Jess – See ehn .. Im even becoming dark (touching up).. the sun in this town ehn... is not good for my skin.. last year in my school in London .. all those fine boys will be saying .. *"you that cute girl innit?"* (in terrible bristish accent) Because... my skin be glowing .. na abroad skin tone God give from time .. I no sabi how I come be this country citizen wey sun dey bully me anyhow ... anyhow shaa I will update my kit soon..

(a girl with a maroon mini skirt with a big ass enters the office to photocopy a document... Tunde did not even look at her.. he's happily married)

Recipient – You know what? let me transfer you some funds .. use it to update your wardrobe and make up kit .. big sister got you.. you know say me I no dey work na husband money I dey chop ..my problem is how to spend it

(Drops call .. Jess's phone beeps with a text message)

"It was a Credit alert 50,000 ..... her Account balance 80,000

(displays on screen)

Jess – Cheeeei...(Tunde turns to her) I've gotten alert ...

Tunde – (Speaks lowly) you are in an office o .. keep it low

Jess – (Eyes him) hater .. ive just gotten an alert .. when was the last time you got an alert? Salary day ehn.. last month??? (laughs hysterically..Tunde just looking)

(Tunde picks up his phone and placed a call through to the Bank Manager... Jess hisses and turns back to her desk reluctantly picking up a document.. to read)

(manager picks)

Bank Manager – Ah.. Mr Tunde... how do you do today?

Tunde – im tight.. business is moving just as fine

Bank Manager– I'm sure you are calling back because you saw my missed call?

Tunde – Yes ... as a matter of fact

Bank Manager –I just want to thank you for this boy ... Tim.. no no no no ... that boy is electric .. that boy na wizard o ... he just repaired my Laptop that my ICT guys have been collecting money from me for .. he didn't even buy any hardware or hard disk or anything like that... ha ..thank you oo

Tunde – well.. Thank God .. im glad you guys can work together ... yess .. you know.. I was thinking... maybe we can hangout ..... tomorrow evening .. you know after work .. bills on me (Jess turns to Tunde in disbelief)

Bank Manager – oh.. how nice... great idea .. oh wait .. whats tomorrow?

Tunde –uhmm... Thursday .. we can do after work.. or friday?

Bank Manager – im not really sure though.. I will call you tomorrow evening , I will tell Tim too.. I don't even know if the boy can hang out till late .. i don't want to spoil that boy

Tunde – Na malt he go drink now (both laughs) oya now

Bank Manager – Cheers

Tunde – yeah till tomorrow (drops phone)

(Scene changes to Bank)

Tim – (talking to an unknown female bank staff) my phone is in the Manager's toilet

Unknown staff – no wonder .. I've been calling you .. is it on silent?

Tim – Yes.. as a matter of fact

Unknown staff -I want you to photocopy the bank's manifest... I need a copy

Tim – Ok Madam ..

(Tunde's office)

Tunde and Jessica are making out profusely ... kissing ...gagging .. in rush to get each other naked ... they went towards a mini printer .. printer falls on the ground .. paper scatters on the floor ... making a loud sound .. catches attention of other staff in other office .. they couldn't see what was going on inside...Jess and Tunde's office is exclusive to them... They struggled to get to the door .. Tunde locks the door.. switches off one light .. leaving one light on... at this time Tunde was on singlet .. his shirt and tie roughandled on the floor ... Jess's cloth on the floor ... she has just her brazier on.. ... ... Jess lies down on the table.. office table ... Tunde was focused... doing it... Jess making sounds..office people hearing strange noise ... they move closer to the door .. to confirm if it what they think... it was what they were thinking ..

Tunde is giving it hard to Jess.. in the Office.. at 2:30Pm... no one dared to knock ... Tunde is seen covering Jess's mouth, he retorted *"don't shout .. don't shout we are in the office..."* Tunde is sweating mad!

outside the office, like 3 people were seen close to the door, Toyosi was among them... listening ... noise reduces.... Silence .... Dead silence........(people outside returns back to their duty post)

Jess – (whispering) what just happened? (Using one hand to cover her breasts)

Tunde – (sweaty) I swear I don't know ... you see...(goes back to switch the light on) (whispering) .... I will want this .. this thing that just happened right now ... to be very discreet.. don't tell anybody (picks up his shirt and tie from the floor) see i will give you 50k to keep quite

Jess – (still whispering) 50k? are you mad? Am a married woman...I live under a man's roof...plus ... I think they heard ... (pointing at the door.. pretends to cry)

Tunde – (Looks at her sternly) you think so?.. yee! I am doomed ...(picks up the printer and papers back to the table... gives Jess her cloth and bra.. she wears her clothes)

Jess – we didn't even use condom.. (Tunde looks at her)

(Silence .... Dead Silence ....)

(both of them tried to dress to look as "well put together" as the way they were looking before the incident)

Jess – see ehn.. me I cant stay here.. im going home

Tunde – yeah .. me too

Jess What? We can't go out the same time?

Tunde – oh .. okay ..

Jess – (tries and open the door.. realizes the door is locked .. looks at Tunde) you even locked.. mtsheew... (hisses)

(the noise from trying to open the door got the other staff's attention)

Jess – (turns the key once walks out of the office confidently with her shabby make up... other staff fakes concentration on other things)

Tunde – (after a shortwhile.. Tunde comes out his office.. locks the door with key and walked out of the office with his head hung upon his neck with his badly arranged tie ... a woman at the reception claps (inaudible) her hands sarcastically)

(Scene rewinds fast to when Tunde drops the call with Bank Manager)

(30 minutes earlier...)

Tunde – Na malt he go drink now (both laughs) oya now

Bank Manager – Cheers (drops phone)

Tunde – yeah till tomorrow (drops phone)

(jess turning her chair fully facing Tunde)

Jess – Ehen ?

Tunde – What?

Jess – wonders shall never end ... so you are taking some people out? With which money?

Tunde – (acting cocky) I mean .. that's what I do In my quite time.. for my sober reflection... giving back ..

Jess – (interjects) heyysss.... Who are you lying to? Me ? (showing him hand that she cant be deceived) everybody knows you are stingy .. as in .. you are soo stingy I'm surprised I still talk to you..

Tunde – Haan .. its not that bad now

Jess – Its that bad oo.. lets stop talking about it and face our work (jess faces her desk)

Tunde – (Tunde pauses ... startled.. didn't know what to say) You know what? That same tomorrow after work .. I will also take you out.. I will take all of you out...

Jess – Abegi .. take me out? (scoffs) You cannot afford where I eat.. don't worry, I don't want someone to faint or asking for price of everything before they pay... besides I don't want you to go bankrupt... I rather take myself out.. my husband is out of town

Tunde – reason why I can take you too out.. your husband is not in town (laughs) chai .. (shaking his head) I've suffered... let me show you something (brings out his phone)

(walks towards jess to show her his account balance to read **N5, 199,900**.. Displays on screen)

Jess – (speechless... looks up to Tunde in disbelief .. sniffs Tunde's perfume .. asks) what perfume are you wearing?

Tunde – (answers casually) I wear designer perfumes only (still standing by Jess) so.. next time, before you say someone is stin ... (notices Jess still staring at him) .. what?

Jess – its just that... ive not seen someone so discreet about their worth.. (... licking her lips ... they start admiring some qualities about themselves and charging against each other)

(Beginning of sex scene replays .. fades out)

Chapter Four

Tunde gets home .. Ireti setting the dining table ...

Ireti - Hey babe .. how was work?

Tunde – Fine   fine!

(wallclock time moves fast from 7:30pm to 8:30am in the morning... day break)

Ireti – aren't you going to work today .. its morning ... u are not even considering the traffic...

Tunde – meh.. I will just call in sick .. I'm tired mehn...uhhmm.. please take Daisy to school...I don't think I will go anywherr... I... (yawns) .... I might just go to the bank later maybe .. you know... chill out with the guys..

Ireti - I don't understand, you are not going to work cus you are sick ... but you will still chill out with guys later?

Tunde – You don't understand... its not everytime work..work work!!!... you can make strong connections at social gatherings.. see... I'm a millionaire now .. I need to mingle with millionaires to double the income .. you know I don't play (acting cocky).. so in essence ...thats what I wanna do with this week's Thursday.. which coincidentally ...is today ... SO .. thank you ....don't be late to work... love you!..

Ireti – love you too .. bye! Daisy.. come lets go.. (Daisy follows her out of the house.. with a toy in her hand)

Tunde – Bye sweetie

Ireti – (talking to Daisy..) say bye Daddy..

Daisy – (could barely speak) bye bye "thatdy"..

(Tunde smiles... looks at wall clock . time says 8:45am .. goes to the fridge.. brings out a hot drink and a cup ... plays music ... relaxing in front of the TV.. as he was about to change channel ....Nepa takes light...power outage)

Tunde - Chai.. nawa oo .. today ... today ..that I want to relax

(he picks up a plastic chair and makes his way outside the house wearing a singlet and relaxes there.. he receives text message on his phone from Jess)

(Jess's message displays on screen) "Please yesterday never happened.. lets keep it that way"

Tunde - Typing... (on screen) we shouldn't be texting ourselves .. (he only typed this .. after a second thought .. he cancelled it) and Typed ... "Ok" and sent)

Tunde –*Typing* (on screen)... please delete your last text.. no texting please!!!!!!!!!!!!!!

(Another text from Jess)

Jess – "Ok"

Tunde – (tired .. she doesn't seem to get the message.. says ..) which kind wahala be this ?

Time goes from 9'am to 3'o clock pm in the afternoon

(Screentime displays 3'o clock digitally)

Tunde enters his bathroom to take his bath

A fat unknown character enters another bathroom to take his bath

Tunde comes out of the bathroom and enters into his bedroom with towel on

The unknown character enters a bedroom also with towel to meet two other guys and a girl

Tunde wears a native attire .. sprays D&G perfume like 6 times on himself

Unknown character wears a black turtle neck with red patch on his shoulders

(unknown character's face hasn't shown since.. even till this point, unknown characters co hort's faces are still hidden)

Tunde wears his wrist watch

Unknown character wears black gloves

Tunde wears his shoes

Unknown character wears All stars chuck taylor's tennis shoes

Tunde picks up his phone and car keys

Unknown character picks up his gun and cartridge .. fixes it and cocks his gun

Tunde faces mirror speaks to himself

Tunde - its about time.. its gonna be a lit night (feeling himself)

Unknown character - (faces the rest..starts talking ...all are now on black masks)

its about time ... (points finger) its gonna be a lit night (funny accent) .. I need you all to stick to plan (the remaining gang members nod in agreement... all of them with guns)

(Tunde drives out of his house)

Gets to a Supermarket

(Tunde buys a bottle of Baileys and 8 sachets of plantain chips... enters his car and continued his journey... eating the chips)

Camera stays with Tunde .... He has driven for about 30 minutes (he is now in a bit of a busy traffic)

He picks up his phone

Dials Bank Manager's number

(sounds of Manager's phone ringing from Tunde's end)

(Manager Picks)

Bank Manager – "Mr Tunde" ... "Mr Tunde.... Is that you"?

Tunde _ Yes Managerial duties .. it is me .. im ready now .. are we not hanging out again?

Bank Manager – what? Mr. Tunde .... (Manager gets distracted talking to someone else " wait wait "telling the person he was talking to) let me tell this man maybe he can call the police.. yes Mr. Tunde .. yes please can you call the police?

Tunde – police ? ha ha.. whats happening?

Bank Manager – yes there has been a robbery.. just now they even killed four people! Ive been trying to call the police all their numbers are not going through?! I don't know.. can you call any police at all you know.. Tazzrev bank ..the one in eleventh street..

Tunde – what? a robbery? Four people? What are you sayi...? wait... did they go with the money?

Bank Manager – yes nooow.. it's a robbery! (phone line getting distorted) please .. "call the police".... (in distortion).. they came with a black Hyundai car .. with plate number LKJ 121 AB

Tunde – with my 5million?

Bank Manager – all the bank money... at least 125 million (Distortion...)

Tunde – Hello ! .... Hello !!

(Line cuts)

Tunde – (alarmed) My 5 Million .... Let me call the DPO..

(on screen ... dialing..... DPO from contacts)

scene rewinds fast ...

(30 minutes earlier)

The front of the bank, about 5 people on a queue by the atm machine... a customer approached the entrance ..Bank security with a metal detector.. scans her

Bank Security – you are welcome to Tazzrev bank

Customer – thank you (enters bank... another customer leaves bank)

Bank Security – have a nice day (talking to the one leaving)

At this time ... a black tinted glass Hyundai car pulls over to the gate of the bank.. the gate of the bank is closed with a security with a gun just by the side and another security stationed to open the gate ... so the Hyundai moved forward and waited..

Inside the black Hyundai

Girl Robber – (in mask.. sitted in the front sit) hey ... (talking to the driver) don't be in a rush (speaks slowly) wait for the right time..

A blue Honda comes in front of the bank .. the security stationed at the gate goes to the trunk.. opens it and signaled the security with the gun to open the gate.

Just as the gate was opened for the Blue Honda to drive in ... the Hyundai reverses and enters the gate of the bank .. parking the car in a way the gate can no longer be closed

The securities at the gate were taken aback and they became curious who could drive like that ... especially around a banking premises.

Everything pauses ..

In slow motion ...

The gate security is seen holding his gun firmly but pointed to the ground and looking at the car with suspicion

(Inside the bank)

The bank manager in the bank speaking to one of the staff on intercom

Tim seated in front of his computer with his earpiece on

A customer receiving her cash and putting it in her bag

(outside the bank)

Everything in split seconds..

Girl Robber – Now!

Three doors of the Hyundai jacks open at the same time remaining only the driver.. the driver reverses the car backwards fast and suddenly.. the three doors opening closes at the same time

The armed bank security at the gate realizes they are armed robbers tries to point his gun... the unknown character with the red patch shoots the armed security at the gate on his foot first with his automatic pistol.. security falls on the ground and puts 2 more bullets in his body, killing him instantly .. without hesitation

With sounds of gunshots, everybody in and around the bank premises disperses.. shouting ... panicking .. including the unarmed security at the gate who took to his heels totally disappearing away from the bank

(inside the bank)

Everyone being alerted, running helter skelter .. Manager is seen confused.. not knowing what to do, Tim removes his earpiece looking left and right ...looking for where to hide

(Outside)

the 3 other armed policemen stationed in strategic positions.. strategizing .. but seemed confused also... they manage to get themselves ready by cocking their Ak 47s ... slowly so as to make less noise.. and not attract the robbers with their sounds

(one of the policemen..)

Policeman – (whispering on his walkie talkie) request for back up! Robbery at Tazzrev ... request for backup!! (distortion continues till radio slowly goes off....!) chai... battery (removes battery... puts it back ... hits the radio to see if it will respond ... it didn't)

(The 3 armed robbers are in their hiding positions.. except for the one in the car .. by the gate.... The female robber signals the one with a red patch on his shoulders..)

Girl Robber – Now! Now!! Now!!! ... its go time! (2 robbers leaves their hiding places moving swiftly with their heads down to another hiding positions)

The policemen starts shooting the moving robbers ... approximately like 8 shots, they missed throughout

In another split seconds .. the robber with a red patch , comes out in slow motion ... making distracting skills confusing the police and single-handedly killing the 3 armed policemen.. with just his pistol, including the one calling for back up

All armed security men at the bank are now neutralized ... 4 policemen dead!

All hiding robbers come out of their hideouts and properly conduct their business... the one with the red patch .. drags out the security who was initially with the metal detector from his hiding place , points his gun to his head and orders him to open the bank door

In cinematographic effects/ slideshows

(Inaudible)

Bank manager on his knees with his hands up with the Lady robber shouting at him (inaudible)

Bank customers all lying down

Robber with a red patch on his shoulders sitted on the counter .. looking left and right (calmly no pressure whatsoever)

The supporting robber once had a vespa bike is seen slapping a male bank staff

Tim on the ground shaking ..

Old bank customer gasping for breath as if she's about to die

Robber with the red patch still sitted, calmly.. looking left and right

Camera shows Female robber pointing her gun to the Bank manager and with a random bank customer .. headed for the safe room, she shouts...

Girl Robber - MOVE!!! (inaudible.. remember its in split seconds and cinematographic effects)

Female robber gives the manager and the customer 4 big black travelling bags.. Bank manager and the customer clears up the vault stocking all the money in the bags with her gun to their heads. The Robber with the red patch comes into the vault and picks up two bags .. the other robber comes In and picks up the other two bags with some cash flying all around.. the female robber covers them as they exit the bank... the cash into the trunk of their Hyundai ... which reversed immediately into the traffic, in a bid to escape.. Disappears almost immediately

(Inside the bank)

Bank Manager- Im doomed ... Armed robbers ... are you okay ? are you okay (asking the staff and customers).. where is my phone ? (checks for his phone in his pockets... dials it)

"Dialing Police on screen"

Response – **"**Sorry the number you trying to call is not reachable**"**

(The bank manager still in shock ... looking around and trying to help and console traumatic customers and staff)

Bank Manager's Phone starts ringing ...

(Tunde on phone)

Bank Manager – "Mr Tunde" ... "Mr Tunde Is that you"?

Movie Fastforwards back to Tunde was calling the DPO

Chapter Five

A bungalow in a compound is seen with sign post in front with (Iya Dunni Motels "for your outstanding pleasure and "torisim")

The song "my darling" by Tiwa Savage playing in the background

A set of well dressed women with high makeup lurking around the premises ..

(In one of the rooms)

time tells 4'o clock pm

The DPO is seen sitted on the couch of the motel with a bottle of lager by his side... (smoke coming out of his cigarette) his police shirt is unbuttoned ... his protruding belly is round and conspicuous in his sparkling white singlet ..He picks up his jar of beer to have a gulp.. Bathroom door opens, His mistress steps out of the bathroom with white towel, another white towel weaved around her head for her hair..

DPO – my darling bebe.... my love for yo..... (lady interjects)

Mistress – Ssshhhh (put her index finger on her mouth) ... don't say anything... I'm about to take you on a ride to the heavens ...tell me... are you ready? (puts one leg on the handle of the couch the DPO is sitting on... dropping the white towel on her body... camera shows her from the back ... butt naked)

DPO – you know what? I am born ready ... (removes his wedding ring ..)

Mistress – Daddyyy... that's why I love you.. you are a gentleman (smiles)

(DPO rushing to remove his clothes ...... his phone starts ringing.... "Tunde *calling*")

Mistress – OoooH! Why is your phone distrub... (picks up DPO's phone ..)

DPO – HEY!! Don't hang up .... Just put it on silence (smiles at her)

(Camera back at Tunde)

Tunde – damn! ... he's not picking ... DPO now.. haba..

(back in the motel .... J Holiday "Bed" playing in the background)

DPO and his mistress starts ... kissing ... smiling and laughing as they lay on the bed .. slow..ly

Camera back at Tunde.. still driving ... looking at his phone frantically and trying DPO's number ...he then gets to a mild traffic .. A BLACK HYUNDAI pulls up to his side ... he notices it... faces front.. looking at his phone to see if DPO will pick his call... then the car overtakes him, enters his front.. he notices the plate number LKJ 121 AB

(flashback of **Bank Manager** talking to Tunde on phone ..In the bank)

Bank Manager - ... yes nooow.. it's a robbery! (phone line getting distorted) please .. "call the police".... (in distortion).. they are in a black Hyundai car .. with plate number LKJ 121 AB

Tunde's eyes is seen wide open upon realization that the armed robbers are right in front of his car!!

He comes to the side of the car and tries to get a hint of what they look like... he couldn't, because the windows are tinted... so he decides to follow them wherever they were going... without them noticing ofcourse

So ..

Hyundai takes a left turn

Tunde takes a left turn

Hyundai overtakes like 3 cars

Tunde overtakes the 3 cars

Hyundai takes a right turn

Tunde takes a right turn

(In the Hyundai... the driver looking at his side and rear mirror)

Robber's Driver – Most belli ... you see that car behind us .. he's been following us

(none of the robbers had their masks on at this time... Most Belli turns back to see)

Most belli – (he's the one with the red patch on his shoulders all along) ehen ? you sure about this?

Robber Driver – I can't be more sure

Most belli – from the bank?

Robber Driver – I.... I don't think so

Most belli – ha .. ha (surprised) well then.. lose him..

Robber Driver – alright then.. (starts driving skillfully... and carelessly)

Tunde – (tries to follow up the driving.. but couldn't)

the Hyundai makes an abrupt turn.. few seconds later Tunde makes the same turn, but could no longer find the black Hyundai

(in the Hyundai... they can see as Tunde's car passes by where they were hiding)

Most belli – every one , mask on! (they all put on their masks.... faces driver) I want a drive by

(In Tunde's car)

Tunde – (lost) ... where are they? (the Hyundai suddenly appears boxing him in.. nowhere to go)

A chubby guy (Most belli) gets out of the Hyundai ... pointing his gun straight to Tunde's head ... furious.. he intended to kill him

(Tunde hands up... knowing he is trouble)

Most belli – Get the fuck out of the car!

Tunde – Please.. please.. don't shoot me.. (as he makes his way out of the car with his hands up looking down)

He seems to recognize Tunde from somewhere.. removes mask to see if Tunde will recognize him... he didn't

Tunde – (looks up to the Robber) please don't kill me ... its because of my money with you guys ... that's why I'm following you .. please (almost crying)

Most belli- what? Your money? You own the bank ?

Tunde – no sir! I don't ... but... i.... I have my money with them.. my 5 million is with them ... but now with you ... please just give me ... I will stop following you

Most belli – what? You must be really stupid .. as a matter of fact .. you are lucky I haven't put a bullet in your head already

Tunde – im sorry sir... its just that.. its my... (interjects)

Most belli – shut up! ... (in disbelief) you look educated .. are you a graduate?

Tunde – Yes .. yes Sir

Most belli – what did you study?

Tunde - I am a Quantity surveyor

Most belli – then you should know we didn't steal your money, rather we didn't steal any money from you ... we stole from the bank (scratches his head and speaks to himself..) "I cant believe I'm doing this.." (faces Tunde) your money is still with the bank ... because your money (wants to explain more but gives up when ... (the driver horns the car... and says...)

Robber driver – (calls him) Most belli...(the robber sitting in front with the driver looks at him at the mention of the name) ..we gotta go.. (most belli looks back...masked robber driver signals him its time to go)

Most belli - once again ..(pointing his gun at Tunde) you are lucky ... you are actually lucky because on a normal day I would have shot you .. today .. I prepared only for 4 people   .. I don't want to make it 5

Tunde – O.. ok Sir .. thank you sir

(Most belli enters Hyundai and zooms off)

(In the Hyundai ...)

Girl Robber – what are you doing Most belli ? that guy saw your face..

Most belli – don't worry , that guy is too stupid to know anything

Girl Robber – (looking at most belli ... she is surprised he didn't kill Tunde)

Most belli– (notices the look) what? You want me to talk to him .. and kill him?

Girl Robber – he was following us .. you didn't have to talk to him, the stakes are high on today's gig !!

Most belli – well .. I spoke to him … as a matter of fact I educated him on something .. so I couldn't kill him .. you get? … I mean…. What will I gain if I kill my student? Rather … what will I gain … if I speak with someone on something important .. and I still go ahead and shoot him? … that will be a waste of my precious time talking with him.. because… only the dead will know what was said… that doesn't make any sense .. I like to teach … the living … not the dead … you get the logic ?

Robber at passenger side – Most belli the boss! Too much brains!!! Chai … baba we are Rich now … (all robbers bursts into laughter … hysterically)

(Back to Tunde… outside his car .. where Most belli left him.. pressing his phone)

His account details shows on screen to read "N5,199,000"

Tunde gives a sigh of relief (looking up) thank God he says, he opens his car door, his phone starts ringing.. he brings out the phone from his pocket

"DPO calling"

Tunde – huh… its now this one is one is calling (stares at the phone for a while .. picked) Hello sir… can you hear me?

DPO – (mistress resting on his chest) Hello.. my son I've not heard from you in a while since that your case.. I worked tediously on that case .. we couldn't unravel the suspects.. but investigation is still on going (mistress goes and light a stick of cigarette)

Tunde – Huh .. not that at all .. I wanted to tell you before that..

DPO – That what?

Tunde – I spoke with Tazzrev Bank manager .. and he was like there was a robbery

DPO – what? Robbery?

Tunde – Yes o ... I even heard they killed four people and they robbed a bank ..NO .. no ...they robbed the bank and killed four people .. I don't know how it happened sha cos I wasn't there.. but I know they robbed a bank and killed four people (casually).. but coincidentally (.........SILENCE) .. I happened to see them .. you know in traffic... in a black Hyundai .. so I followed them

DPO – (listening attentively)

Tunde – one of them even told me I was lucky he didn't put a bullet in my head..

DPO – were you together?

Tunde – Yes ,. few minutes ago.. I even saw one of their faces ..(laughs) can you imagine? stupid armed robbers (laughs)

DPO – where are you? Let me come and meet you..because I need to protect you.. those robbers may realize it's a mistake they let you live .. they may come back for your head, so let me just come and meet you and we'll sort everything out, stay where you are I will come and meet you.

Tunde – Ok .. if that's how you want it..

(Few Minutes later)

(DPO arrived with 2 prado jeeps, 6 policemen came with the DPO .. on Highlighting from the vehicles, DPO starts giving instructions)

One policeman with a camera start snapping everywhere the DPO points (all was around Tunde)

DPO – secure the perimeter.. (points at his men)

DPO – (on radio) I want you to stop and search every black car within oba bridge... Takewon junction and moduvea avenue Over ...

On radio – roger that over!

(In Black Hyundai)

The robber sitted in the passenger sit in front is seen with an old transmitter radio with a wire to its antenna and to an iphone with a frequency application listening to DPO's instruction...

Old transmitter radio – (distorted sounds but clear in the end) " I want you to stop and search every black car within oba bridge... Takewon junction and moduvea avenue Over ... – roger that over"

Male Robber – (looks at the rest)

(inside a supermarket)

Man – (talking to the attendant) take this 2 dispenser water to my car outside.. it's a white Toyota Corrolla ..

Attendant – (arranging the dispenser bottles on a trolley) parked where?

Man – you will see it .. its close to the entrance (pointing his remote to unlock the car... car not visible from his position)

Attendant – okay .. (heads towards the car with the Trolley)

Man – Please my change .. (talking to the cashier)

Cashier – uhm ... there is no... or do you have 200 let me give you 500?

Man – kai... you people ... let me check ... (puts hand in pocket.. brings out his wallet.. removes money gives to the cashier .. cashier gives him 500)

Attendant – (couldn't find his car) Sir .. no white corolla outside ...

Man – (laughs) you are not serious ... mtscheew... Lets go (heads outside with a white polythene bag containing more items he bought from the supermarket)

(On getting outside ... the only car parked is a black Hyundai... the man kept on looking at his car key ... and pressing the remote... as if that will make the car reappear)

(back to Tunde and DPO)

DPO – (faces Tunde) Yes .. my friend .. did you say you saw their faces?

Tunde –No.. just one of them .. he said I was lucky he didn't kill me

DPO – (looks at him sternly.. bursts into laughter) Arrest this man..(talking to his men)

One policeman jumped and caught Tunde as if he was about to run .. they both fell on the ground and quickly put handcuffs on Tunde's hands

Another Policeman with a paper start reading...

Policeman - "FREEZE!!!....... You are under arrest .....U have the right to remain silent .. everything you (stammers) everythin.. you you say will be used against you in the court of law .. you also.... Also... have a right to lawyer."

Tunde – what? oGa DPO.. will you allow this to happen to me ? just like that? Im not a suspect.. what are you people saying ?

(A Checkpoint)

(The robbers are seen without a mask in a white Corrolla arriving at a checkpoint.. "tease me" by wizkid playing over the radio)

All black cars around are parked .. commuters are being interrogated, The white corolla approaches the road block.... A Policeman bends to look inside of the car ... Most belli's hand stationed on the trigger hidden from the police

Police – Yes .. reduce that music (driver tries to reduce music .. seems confused .. took like like 5 seconds to reduce music)

Robber driver – yes officer?

Police - where to?

RD – we .. we are going to a friends party

Police – (looks at everyone in the car for like 5 seconds…) be careful out there … its not safe.. have a nice night (signals them to pass)

RB – Thank you sir

White Corrolla passes checkpoint

Radio attached to the police – a "642" car theft .. there has been a report of a stolen car … a white Corrolla.. include that in your search over! (the policeman didn't seem to bother about the announcement because the next car he is about to search is black)

Black car driver – whats the meaning of this?? Why the road block ??? ehn?

Police – calm down ..calm down

Black car driver – do you know who I am ?? do you know who I am ??

Police – Sir .. I say calm… infact come down … come and open your booth

Black car driver – (revs his car twice… 3 policemen stand alert .. point their guns at him) ok ok … (puts his hands up … comes out of his car.. goes to his trunk and opens it) You see .. you see.. there is nothing there… you know what? (points finger at the,) this time tomorrow .. you are no longer in the force… you don't know who you are messing with..

(DPO's Office)

DPO – you mean.. (shouting at the remaining 6 police officers that followed him to arrest Tunde .. angry) .. I will be the first policeman in this state.... to know that there was a robbery in a bank .. that they count scores? Im not surprised .. you are all useless.. im the only vibrant policeman you people have in this state....I'm an embodiment of smartness and agility.. I don't just open my mouth to talk.. unless its important (pointing finger) ....unlike you.. Do you even know this work? I wonder what they teach in police college these days... Do you know the amount of intelligence I had to put in to be able to arrest our only suspect? (referring to Tunde) A robbery of this gravity occurred In my very own division....No! we have to hold somebody responsible

I heard the Governor is interested in this case...I must have something to tell the commissioner when he calls me ...I'm in a more fix than you people.. and till now .. you incompetent people haven't still done anything .. seem where is Steven?

Kamoru- he will resume by 6

DPO – ok ... its 5:30 .. you see .. if you people know what you are doing... Steven will be at work by now .. this kind of case happened at your division.. and he is still in his house .. all of you .. you can go .. is that press guy around?

Kamoru – Let me check sir .. (goes and comes back) yes he has come ..

(Tunde House)

Tunde's wife (Ireti) is seen arranging the dining .. news on TV caught her attention

Breaking News ..

Police arrest suspect linked to Tazzrev Bank robbery

(DPO is seen with 3 policemen behind him on TV)

Tunde sitted on the ground in DPO's background with another person with one locally made pistol in front of them

DPO - You see .. on the right .. is the suspect linked to the bank robbery where 4 policemen died this afternoon .. on the left is one guy that doesn't talk much .. we don't know who he is yet.. but he was arrested with the gun...

(Jess is seen also watching TV ... sitted on a couch .. with a surprised face....her husband in the background pressing clothes)

Jess's Husband – isn't that your work guy? Whats his name again ? Tunde

Jess – Shhh...

Jess's Husband – stingy Tunde (laughs) I don't know they arrest people for being stingy these days (Jess looks at him somehow)

DPO on TV-.. that's not the point now .. investigation is still ongoing .. you need to see the way I was able to intercept the criminal.. but that's a story for another day .. report any suspicious movements around you to the police and we will ensure to keep you safe.... (smiles to the camera)

Ireti – (In disbelief.. throughout... tears rolling down her cheeks .. Daisy is not there)

Back to the station

Press guy interviewing DPO – Cut!

DPO – how did I do?

Press guy – fantastic

DPO – hmm ...(walking away from the press guy towards the entrance of the police station) ... I know ...I know I look good... by the time my bebe loves see me on TV ..

(laughs) not even the babies .. if commissioner see me for TV.. na once he go approve my promotion

Steven – Evening Sir

DPO – so you .. its now you are coming? No need sef.. see that man.. (pointing at Tunde on the floor) he is the suspect .. meet one of them (pointing at police) to give you the gist .. after lets have a meeting.. I'm leaving soon .. so make it fast

Steven – Ok sir

DPO – put him in the cell when you are done with him

(DPO's Office... "DPO means Divisional Police Officer")

(Inspector Steven enters DPO's office... a "wanted" chart is seen on DPO's wall identifying the name Most belli as number one on the watch list and Kingpin but no picture, only a question mark...indicating uncertainty. There are other speculations around the sketch)

DPO – now.. they have briefed you abi?

Steven – yes Sir

DPO – I want you on this case... handle it with caution .. I want you to give me something by tomorrow morning .. four policemen died .. under my watch .. get as much information as you can from him.. we need to arrest the others.. just give me something tomorrow..

Steven – ok sir

(DPO's phone starts ringing)

"Commissioner calling"

DPO signals Steven to go out of his office

Commissioner – Hello .. Mensa

DPO – My honorable commissioner sir.. I am humble sir

Commissioner – whats wrong with you? You are smiling ? on TV? when we have 4 policemen dead... on your watch!

DPO – im sorry sir ... I didn't mean it like that .. at least on the bright side ... we have a suspect

Commissioner – Yes about that suspect .. I know him... I know that guy

DPO – yes .. you know him?

Commissioner – Yes now .. have you forgotten we did his case together that time? That I headed the team?

DPO – yes... yes .. I remember .. chai.. but we cant release him oo.. hes the only one that has at least admitted to seeing the Robbers' face

Commissioner – ehen? Ha .. okay oo .. the Governor is on my neck

DPO – don't worry we will try our best .. But sir.. Hope you haven't forgot that my promotion we spoke about?

Commissioner – 4 people dead, not just 4 people, 4 policemen... during a bank robbery and you are there talking about promotion.. if you like don't do your job, you will see what I will personally do to you (Cuts call)

(Evening of the Following day)

Tunde's face battered, he was allowed to see his wife

Tunde – Ireti .. I need a lawyer, a very good one .. what these people have put on my head.. I don't just understand .. do you know (looks if the stationed police is listening to their conversation) they made me confess to the crime? (whispers)

Officer – heeyyysss... speak up... no whispering.. infact you have one minute left

Ireti – (Sobbing) I will .. I will get you a good lawyer .. don't worry about that (tears roll down her cheeks)

Tunde – see … I don't need you to cry, I need you to be strong, this is the devil's work .. im sure very soon .. everything will be ok ..God will vindicate me… I just need you to get me a good criminal lawyer … do you understand?

Ireti – yes , I do .. Daisy said I should say hi

Tunde – (with a sad face) tell Daisy I love her… that daddy will be back soon, tell her I will take her to amusement park when I get back .. ok? Please don't bring her here, you understand me? Ehen..

Officer – time up… (officer picks him up and back to the cell)

Following day same scene and setting as the last, ireti with a changed cloth… a pack of fast food and a bottle of lucozade in front of Tunde as he eats furiously.. he was very hungry

Ireti – I met a good lawyer this morning .. my boss recommended him

Tunde – ehen? That's good.. so why is he not here with you?

Ireti – he said he will not come to the police station until we deposit 50% his professional fee

Tunde – ok .. so how much? (Drinking his lucozade)

Ireti – 2 million

Tunde – (spits a little of his lucozade .. starts coughing… the liquid choked him.. he coughs for like 30 seconds, he finally catches his breadth .. little tears in his eyes.. he cleans it with the tissue) haba! 2 million?

(Scene Changes .. same spot .. just with lawyer.. no officer)

Tunde – Haba! 2 million? Lawyer … did I kill person?

Barrister – its funny .. you are asking me .. I should be asking you … because the police and the general public thinks you were among those robbers, so until you tell me something to the contrary .. I'm afraid .. to me you are a suspect

Tunde – ofcourse Not … I didn't kill anybody , I have a job, I am a responsible man with a wife and kid .. why will I jeopardize all that and decide to be an armed robber?

Barrister – well … why then did you confess?

Tunde – see .. Barrister … the reason I have agreed to pay you 2 million naira which I already paid 50%

"Account balance on screen reads N4, 199,000"

Tunde - (raising his voice) is for you to get me out of this mess... someone is trying to frame me up (whispering)

Barrister – see today is Saturday .. they will not grant you bail … at least not until Monday when they take you to court .. then I will apply for your bail, the chances of the judge granting you bail on that day is very slim…. The offences they are charging you for is iron clad. I together with my team will try our best and as for the statement you made under duress… we will know what to do with that at trial…ok?

Tunde – thank you … thank you Barrister

Chapter Six

A signpost is seen with the inscription "Court in session .. KEEP QUITE!" outside the court room.

A Cameraman is seen with a Reporter

Reporter – "Today is the trial of Tunde Ajisafe one of the armed Robbers that robbed Tazzrev bank on the …" (fades out)

(inside the court)

The Court Clerk and Registrar are on their sit, the Court hasn't started sitting yet... armed policemen are in strategic positions, the case is high profile.

Tunde is seen in shackles with a 3 Policemen sitted around him, about 5 lawyers are sitted and discussing silently at the bar while few people are in the gallery, another lawyer walks up to the Registrar. The lawyers are fully robbed.

Among the people at the gallery .. the familiar faces are Tunde's work Manager, Ireti, the Bank Manager wearing a sharp dark blue suit with a dark tie (first time he is seen on suit) sitting at the extreme away from Tunde, Steven dressed in casuals instead of his police uniform.

"3 hard knocks on the Door"

Court Clerk – Court!

All rises as the Judge makes his way to his Chair, takes a bow... everybody takes a bow, Judge sits down, everyone followed suit.

Judge – Good Morning all ..

Lawyers – (chorus) Good morning your lordship

Judge – Registrar, what are you waiting for ?

Registrar – the first case is a criminal case with suit number CCWT 19... between The State versus Tunde Ajisafe

(Tunde stands up and enters a box with inscription "Accused Box" slowly, no longer in cuffs)

Prosecutor Hassan T esq – My Lord we are ready

Registrar – That you Tunde Ajisafe and three others at large on 24th August 2019 conspired and robbed (fades away)

Tunde – Not Guilty

Registrar – Count 2, that you Tunde Ajisafe and three others at large murdered 4 policemen at their point of duty on the 24th... (fades away)

Tunde – Not guilty

Registrar – Count 3 .. That you Tunde ... (fades out)

Tunde – Not Guilty

Defense Counsel – My Lord, now that the Defendant has taken his plea .. we wish to apply for his bail..

Judge – did you hear the charges against the Defendant? it include murder and armed robbery .. you think I will grant your bail application?

Defence Counsel – My Lord, Bail is a constitutional right of the Defendant, he deserves to be heard, whether my Lord will grant it or not will be considered when the application is moved ..

Judge – See see (looking at him from on top of his glasses) .. excuse me Counsel.. the Court will rise for 30 minutes .. when I'm back... both of you will argue the bail application, is that clear?

Lawyers – Yes your Lordship

Judge – the Court will rise

Clerk – Court! (All rise, the Judge steps into his Chambers, everybody sits... the Courtroom became a little disorganized)

Tunde steps out of the dock and meets up with his lawyer ... by the side

Tunde – Do you think the Judge will grant me bail?

Lawyer – we have 50/50 chance .. lets be positive .. okay? everything will be alright

Tunde – Okay .. thank you Barrister

(Tunde goes to sit in the gallery)

the Prosecuting Counsel is seen talking discreetly with the Bank Manager .. the Bank Manager is not on Tunde's side, so he hasn't smiled at him since

Defence Counsel – (talking with another lawyer)

Another Lawyer – Yes.. bail is a constitutional right even when you go deeper into the constitution, you will realize ... (fades out ...vibrating sound starts...)

The vibration continues ... the police sitting beside Tunde is seen bringing out a phone, Tunde's phone ... he was with it all along .....

"Hon Jerry calling"

Police – (Speaking in local language to Tunde) "Egbon.. egba.. phone yin ring" meaning "Your phone is ringing bros"

(gives Tunde the phone)

Tunde – Hon Jerry .. how are you? long time..

Hon Jerry – (he doesn't even know the latest developments about Tunde, he has been in Brazil since their last deal) ha... my friend ..hope you are ok?

Tunde – Yes sir, I am ok

Hon Jerry – Yeah... pleas.. can you come over to my office right away.. come with your Quantity surveyor's seal ... I need you to sign a document for me... a valuation report ... the contractor is right before me.. you remember that Contractor now?

Tunde – Yes yes .. that one we did business together the other time?

Hon Jerry - right .. he has a flight to catch in the next 2 hours to south Africa, he needs you to sign the valuation report .. he is willing to give you 10 million naira ... cash ... just like old times (laughs)

Tunde – what? (caught people's attention.. realizes and speaks in a low voice) I'm coming.. I'm coming

Hon Jerry – Yes! You won't believe he landed another contract in South Africa, he said there's something about you that he likes... don't worry .....come first .....I will give you the gist... we are both waiting for you

Tunde – let me just round up what I'm ... I'll be there .. I'll be there..

(Hangs up and Tunde goes to meet his lawyer, still holding his phone)

Tunde – Uhm .. I will like to see you briefly

Defense Counsel – ok .. hope everything is fine?

Tunde – Yes more than fine .. Please ....could you please call the Prosecuting Counsel for me also, I want to talk with you both

Defense Counsel – discuss it with me first

Tunde – No .. I cant tell you, it has nothing to do with this case (smiles)

Defense Counsel – Ok (goes to call the Prosecuting Counsel)

(The Prosecuting Counsel comes back with Tunde's Lawyer and the 3 of them goes to a side of the Court to discuss)

Tunde – Please .. I'm sorry I had to call this meeting ... something happened that I really have to attend to ... I don't need you people to question me ... but here is what I want you both to do..

(faces Prosecuting Lawyer)

Tunde – when my lawyer applies for my bail, please I don't want you to argue with him...so the Judge can allow.. (Prosecuting Counsel interjects)

Prosecutor Hassan T – (about to become furious)

Tunde – Hold on! let me land.. I am willing to give you both One million Naira, that's Five Hundred Thousand Naira each .. so as to just work as a team ... and let the Court release me on bail... please

Prosecutor Hassan T – (becomes interested) ha har... you didn't tell me it was that ... I thought it was something serious, why not? Okay okay.. so how do you intend to give me the money?

Tunde – I will give you as soon as the Court releases me

Prosecutor Hassan T is seen thinking for about 3 seconds...

The Defense Counsel was curious to know who will break the silence ...

Tunde making awkward gestures to make Prosecuting Counsel agree ..

Prosecutor Hassan T – Uhhm No.. I want it now .. send me the money ..Now Now Now !!!

Tunde – Ok no Problem ... whats your account number , let me transfer

(Tunde starts pressing his phone ... On screen shows "Transfer successful 500,000" 2 times)

Prosecutor Hassan T – (checks his phone .. seems happy) yes I've gotten the alert

Defence Counsel – (checks his phone.... Looks at Tunde ... with disbelief)

Tunde – Thank you gentlemen (Prosecuting Counsel goes back to his sit) you see... (talking with his lawyer) Money makes the world go round.. not this books books and laws you people are quoting (feeling accomplished)

"3 hard knocks on the Door"

Clerk – Court!

All Rise

(Court starts sitting)

the Judge Is seen flipping pages of a file for like 5 seconds

Judge – Yes?

Defence Counsel – Yes My Lord ... before your Lordship is the Bail application of the Defendant, subject to the convenience of this Court, we are ready to proceed

Judge – is the Prosecution ready ?

(Defence Counsel sits down, the Prosecution Counsel stands up)

Prosecutor Hassan T – My Lord .. I'm afraid we are not ready, because if we proceed at this stage, we won't be doing anything in good faith and as a Minister in the temple of justice .. I owe my Country a duty to be truthful always ...

Defence Counsel and Tunde – (Tensed ... both looking at him in disbelief... jaw dropped)

Prosecutor Hassan T – My Lord, Can you believe the Defendant

Defence Counsel – (interjects) My Lord ...

Prosecutor Hassan T – I'm still on my feet.. you cant interject like that ... I'm addressing the Court!

Judge – Defence Counsel (calmly) Defence Counsel ...

Defence Counsel – yes your Lordship

Judge - Sit down .. this is my Court, I coordinate things around here ..yes?

Prosecutor Hassan T – I thank my Lord for the rescue.. my Lord .. as I was saying ...

"audio of what the prosecution was saying playing in the background as a Lady with a veil on her head and dark shades entered the Court... it was Jess"

Jess – (removes her glasses to reveal identity.. sits at the back of the Court)

Prosecution's audio playing in background as Jess enters Court - "My Lord can you believe, the Defendant (points at Tunde) just sent me the sum of Five hundred thousand Naira as bribe, He even gave his own lawyer too another Five Hundred Thousand Naira... making one million Naira ... that I shouldn't contest the bail application.. so he can walk free today

People in Court – (sidetalks and murmuring is heard all around, sound fizzles out later)

Prosecutor Hassan T - My Lord.. can you imagine that? I have the text of the alert I got from Mr Tunde here on my phone as evidence .. if my Lord orders your orderly (police) to check the Defence Counsel's Phone .. My Lord will also see the alert of money just received ... bribery inside the Court of law! That's not permissible! .. My Lord.. not just any Court .. its your court .. the Press are inside this Court as we speak.. what will the public say?

Tunde – (starts crying)

Judge – Is that so?

Defence Counsel – Erm ... Erm

Judge – you know what? Argue your bail application

Defence Counsel – as the Court pleases.. Before your Lordship is a bail application ... (fades out)

Judge – Here is my ruling on the Bail application... Bail refused.... The money offered as bribe by the Defendant to both Counsel in the matter ... the sum of One million Naira is hereby confiscated... Tunde's phone is also confiscated by this Court... The Defence counsel shall seize to appear in this matter and indeed before me as he has encouraged bribery in a Court of law, The Defendant is to be remanded at the maximum correctional facility, I hereby order accelerated hearing...

(Jess notices that their work Manager is also in the gallery but he is sitting in front... she carefully steps out of the Court, she doesn't want him to see her)

Judge – (continues) ... as you all know me, I have zero tolerance for Corruption... that's my Ruling.. this Court shall rise

Clerk – Court! (all rise)

Defence Counsel disappointed with his head down still seated

Tunde with his hands on his head ... blanked out .. standing in the dock .. motionless

(police comes to meet him to take him away.. puts him in cuffs)

(Outside the Court)

Journalists (with audio recorder, phones, microphone) interviewing the Prosecuting Counsel with 2 other lawyers and the bank manager behind him

Reporter – whats your take on today's proceedings?

Prosecutor Hassan T – Yes ... the Court has a discretion, the Court exercised his discretion judicially and judiciously .. thank you (goes away with his entourage)

(The Defence Counsel is seen avoiding an interview)

Reporter – Excuse me Sir .. excuse me Sir

Defence Counsel – No comments ... (hiding his face) No comments .. (as he runs mildly towards his car)

Tunde was put inside a Prison Vehicle and whisked away... remaining the press and other people in the gallery

That Same Night, Tunde is seen on boxers shorts being handed prison uniform by a warden, he wears it.

Tunde could not find a snip of sleep in a cell he shared with 1 other inmate, an old man.

Thoughts of the 10 million Naira he missed kept on ravaging his mind. His cellmate is seen sleeping peacefully with low sound of cricket in the background.

Tunde is heard saying 10 million .. 10 million .. 10 million !!! (quietly)

He tries to remember something ... his account balance (3,199,900 displays on screen)

He stands up .. picks up a small stone from the ground and kept on calculating maths and writing 10, 000, 000 on the wall ... at different places.

(Tunde's House)

Ireti – (goes to turn the TV off) babygirl lets go to bed

Daisy – mummy ...where is thaddy? I want to wait for thaddy (she could barely get those words out of her mouth ... she said it gently)

Ireti – (tears roll down her cheeks.. cleans it quickly) don't worry Daddy will come in the morning

In The Morning

In Prison

Tunde's cellmate is already awake looking at all the calculations on the wall .. he starts wondering

Tunde is asleep

Prison warder with 2 other officers – wake up ... wake up ... we have a lot to do today ... (using his club to make annoying noise on the cell gates)

Cellmate – Hey .. wake up

Tunde – where is my ten million?? (he jacks up)

(Prison Dining)

Prisoners are seen given shabby food .. that looks like beans , but not really beans.. that could not be beans, Tunde is seen in one corner ... with no food .. he was looking at the food with disgust.

Later, the inmates were seen clearing grass... taking it to a place where they will eventually burn them

A prisoner is seen with a cigarette

Another was seen working out .. with 3 others encouraging him

Tunde is seen pushing a wheelbarrow full of grass

He pours the grass where they will burn them

A prison warden approached him,

Warden- "hey.. you have a visitor "

(He leaves the wheelbarrow and follows the warden)

In an office

(Tunde and his wife sitting facing of each other.. Tunde holding a piece of chicken.. eating)

Ireti – I had to pay them .. so they could give us this office .. and for you to have this food you are eating

Tunde – Thank you very much ... I love you baby .. don't worry .. everything will soon be over

A junkie looking Prisoner peeps through the window

Junkie Prisoner – Ha .. Baba ... koda o ... only you just dey here dey enjoy ... baba even me too.. I swear I never chop ..I never chop... Just tell madam to give me small money make I use am skana!! You know ... find my own level (he needs money to get high)

(Tunde stands up from the table .. goes to the window and slides it shut)

Tunde – (still facing the window .. sighs ...)

He turns back to continue his food but his wife is seen standing ... removing her top ... She came to have sex with her husband .. in Prison, desperate times demand desperate measures...

No wonder she had to pay them.

Sex scene happened.

Both of them are relaxed on a couch (Then a knock on the door)

Warden – My friend open the door! What's wrong with you???

Ireti opens the door (smiles at the warden with her shoes in her hand) goes out.

Tunde comes out

Warden – (in pidgin English) I hear say you get money .. but only go dey chop am .. just pray say Court no sentence you, na me you go still come meet... (which means) I heard you have money, but you are stingy .. just pray the Court does not sentence you .. you will eventually end up with me here

Same Night

Tunde is seen sleeping

His cellmate also asleep

Shabby images

"Daisy is seen smiling at Tunde

Images of clouds .. in the night

Moving fast

Then of church

Tunde and Ireti in their wedding cloths - saying "I do"

Images of when Tunde received the 5 million from Hon. Jerry

Random Images

Images of Jess and Tunde sex scene

Images

Images of Tundes wife watching Jess and Tunde sex scene

Images showing Tundes wife holding a knife at her back.. watching them

Shining Knife

Images of Daisy

Tundes wife crying alone

Tundes wife holding a knife up .. angry

Tunde on white suit carrying his daughter Daisy

Tunde behind bars

Tundes wife holding a knife up .. angry (shouts)

Thunder and lighthing on dark clouds

(Tunde wakes up.. grasping for breadth)

(2 Days later in prison)

Ireti – Hey babe .. how are you? (not in a private place)

Tunde – (no answer)

Ireti – ... you look like you've seen a ghost (Ireti laughs.. Tunde smiles)

(Both laughs)

Ireti – hey ... I bought you pineapple ... (puts the food in front of Tunde) – whatever it is .. tell me by this second.. I need to pick Daisy from school

Tunde – alright ... alright ... you see.. you remembered when we got married

Ireti – Yes ?

Tunde – we vowed ... for better or for worse?

Ireti – (hesitates)

Tunde – just say yes .. im getting at something

Ireti – yes?

Tunde – let me j...just cut straight to the chase, I cheated on you ... (both looking straight into each others eyes for 5 seconds .. silence for 5 seconds) I'm sorry

Ireti – Tunde ..? How could you? Tell me.... With who?

Tunde – (looking down) it doesn't matter.. I just want you to forgive and forget

Ireti – (speechless.... And other things girls do when in this circumstances)

Ireti – look .. get this straight (acting crazy) I cant ... and I wont forgive you .. until you tell me with who... with who???

Tunde – Okay okay ... with Jessica .. Jess ..

Ireti – That bitch! And you... how unprofessional .. later u will be saying.. I'm a professional .. I'm a professional ... you cant keep your penis in your trousers.. for someone at work??? (Raises voice)

Tunde – I warned you before now .. don't overreact ... forgive me ..

Ireti – forgive you? Just like that ?? this is too much (burst into tears)

Warden – (notices the wife crying...) okay okay.. time out ..... come and be going ... ushers Tunde back (ireti still sobbing)

Following day

Warden – you have a visitor

(Tunde and Barrister sitting and facing each other)

Barrister – (wearing an orange T shirt with a beautiful young girl wearing a dark gown) We didn't even have the chance to talk after what happened in court the other day

Tunde – (smiles) I saw you running from the press

Barrister – Me? Run? I don't run from battles.. but there are some .. you will have to leave .. not run ... and come back another day well prepared to fight (smiles)

Tunde – Oh that's cool.. I'm surprised you are still on my case ... the judge said you can't be my lawyer again

Barrister – Mr. Tunde .. please before we go further ... I want the balance of one million.. your case is tomorrow.. and its trial .. we cant afford to leave any stone unturned.

Tunde – What? Which one million?

Barrister – (opens a bag he brought .. brings out a document) it says here that ... you engaged me to be your Lawyer till the final determination of your case. (points to a part) look...It says here that you have agreed to pay me the sum of 2 million Naira .. we both signed, I am not here for any dilly dally .. give me my balance

Tunde – (surprised) I'm sorry Barrister .. I'm not paying you

Barrister – I have this document .. I can easily use it to sue you and claim my money .. besides it was your fault .. so don't waste my time

(looking at themselves eye to eye for 5 seconds straight with a straight face....)

Tunde – (bursts into laughter) Barrissster... I'm just testing you (brings out a cheque book from his pocket)

Barrister – so you have your cheque book here with you... ? (writes Barrister a cheque of five hundred thousand Naira.. gives it to Barrister)

Tunde – oh yes .. my loving wife brought it for me yesterday... (Account balance displays 2,699,900 for 5 seconds)

Barrister – oh... (looks at the cheque in a funny way)

Tunde – what is our plan for tomorrow ?

Barrister – Yes .. Mr Tunde meet Susan

Camera focuses on the young girl that came with Barrister

Tunde – (Tunde looks at her...)

Barrister – She will be handling your case henceforth

Tunde – (Tunde looks at Barrister ...looks at the lady... looks back at Barrister) - Barrister.... Why don't you just sentence me to death yourself ? .... You will collect 1.5 million naira from me ... in a case that involves the death of 4 policemen.. and you will send a teenager to be my lawyer ?

Susan – I'm not a teenager

Tunde – (faces her) you are not a teenager ? ok.. tell me .. how old are you ?

Susan – I'm 23 yearsss.. (Barrister interjects)

Barrister – will you sh... (faces Susan) you meet someone for the first time... in a Federal prison and you are telling your age? Hmm? Lawyer ?

Tunde – 23 years old girl??? (in disbelief) sorry ... (faces susan) 23 years old barrister?

Barrister – I need to ask you some questions so we can strategize against your trial tomorrow... are you ready?

Tunde – Yes

Barrister – (faces Susan...) where is your note?

(Susan brings out her jotter and prepares to write)

Barrister – why didn't you go to work .. on the day in question? The day the bank was robbed

Tunde – Barrister .... Long story

Barrister – Long story?? Don't worry we have the time

Tunde – sorry I didn't mean to say that... that day................ I was a bit under the weather ... so I decided to take a day off

Barrister – were you not meant to meet up with the bank manager later that day? Something about having new connections... your wife told me (Susan jotting furiously)

Tunde – see Barrister ... the reason I didn't go to work that day is immaterial to this case .. that's all I can say in answer to your question (scene fades out)

Chapter Seven

(Prosecutor's office, his real name is Hassan T esq.)

Prosecutor Hassan T – (wearing white and black with a corporate cowboy hat) as my star witness in this case .. I intend to treat you specially .. don't worry the DPO will join us soon.. (DPO enters)

DPO – (wearing a conductor suit and papas cap) I'm soo sorry .. it's the traffic..(he closed the door behind him.. 2 police officers mount guard at the door on the other side) I had to tell my boys ... to do the Governor's style .. you know the Governor's style .. sirens (feeling cocky) .. 4 prados .. 2 Hilux .. one ambulance .. all to come and see the Prosecutor and our star witness .. please let it worth my time .. this is a big matter .. I hope you get what am saying? (gesturing money ...nodding and smiling)

Bank Manager – (wearing a suit with no tie.. no hat) Don't worry DPO.. that's a small issue .. at the end of this meeting .. we will go home smiling

(DPO sits down ...Hassan T stands, goes to his shelve where there are many books by the side and brings out a bottle of whiskey pours for himself ... puts whiskey on a tray on another table with 2 glass cups .. didn't offer them.. goes back to his sit with his drink... press a ring beside his chair ... a young girl comes in.. signals her ... She brings the tray to the table in front of them and 4 kolanuts... while all these are happening... DPO audio is playing at the background saying..)

DPO – (Facing Bank Manager) I know there are a lot of grey areas ... but how can a group of armed robbers that killed 4 policemen ... reveal their identity to you .. and not kill you? The funny part .. the way he said it when I called him... ehn.. (mimicking Tunde) ... "they robbed a bank and kill four people" (funny accent)

Prosecutor Hassan T – you called him?

DPO – yes ... he called me first .. I'd get to that later , the story does not just make sense to me .. so I say its better he goes to court, let the court ... based on what we have .. give us judgment .. the souls of the 4 Policeman are crying in the heavens and may not get rest until we get judgment .. so lets do what we can.. to secure a conviction in this matter .. its too much for me to handle.. let the court handle it .. that's life .. when life gives you lemon... make a lemonade .. its not as if I want him to die at all cost, but lets us all do our job (picks up a cup of whiskey and takes a sip.. he squeezes his face)

Prosecutor Hassan T – so Manager .. How do you know Mr. Tunde

Bank Manager – firstly .. I didn't know him personally.. but he maintains an account with the bank ... I got to know him face to face when he deposited a huge amount .. then he started calling... coming to bank unscrupulously.. you know.. as if hes trying to extract information from me .. he even asked one day ..How many armed securities we have.. so since that time, I kept an eye on him .. so I'm not surprised he is found in the middle of all of this

Prosecutor Hassan T – you see .. the reason you are our star witness, is because you were present during the robbery, you know Mr Tunde before the robbery, and he is the suspect in this matter ... we are going to tender the CCTV footage of Tunde at the Supermarket .. the same supermarket ... they stole that man's Corolla .. where they found the Black Hyundai used in the robbery ...my second witness is ofcourse the owner of the Corolla .. you see.. Tunde is not going anywhere, life imprisonment is the least the court will give in this matter

Bank Manager– But the owner of the stolen car did not see Mr Tunde at the supermarket

Prosecutor Hassan T – (looks at him) ehen? How did you know?

Bank Manager– he told me himself , the last time we were in court

Prosecutor Hassan T – you see .. I want you to concentrate on the part of the story.. the part that concerns you... ok ... let me ask ... were you at the supermarket?

Bank Manager – No ..

Prosecutor Hassan T – where were you at the time of the Robbery?

Bank Manager – my workplace

Prosecutor Hassan T – which one is your workplace??

Bank Manager – the Bank

Prosecutor Hassan T – you don't work at the bank! You work at Tazzrev... I want you to be direct ..say Tazzrev Bank.. we are not joking around here ... and don't say anything you did not witness personally... if you do, that will be hearsay evidence and our case can go bad from there ... let me ask you another question

Bank Manager – Ok ?

Prosecutor Hassan T – do you know the owner of the white corolla?

Bank Manager – (thinks for a while ...looks at DPO .. looks at prosecutor answers as if not sure...) No?

Prosecutor Hassan T – of course No! you don't know him.. abi? Do you know him before the robbery?

Bank Manager – No .. no .. not at all... I didn't know that was where you are getting at

Prosecutor Hassan T – So tomorrow be confident .. because we don't know the line of cross examination they are coming with ... by the time we tender his confessional statement through our 3rd witness ... one of the police officers that investigated this matter, our case before the court will be rock solid, iron clad.

(They all smile at themselves in agreement that they are all geared up for the trial)

Bank Manager – Haaa.. don't worry ... like the DPO said .. we all have roles to play. (opens his Brown corporate bag .. brings out 2 cream envelopes and puts them on the table)

Bank Manager - This for you .... And this is for you

DPO – (picks his up his own.... He checks the contents .. he sees hundred dollar bills.. nods his head happily and says) .... You know .. The Governor is interested in this matter .. so when we win ..   it's a win win .. we are getting money ... we will get conviction .. we will certainly get promotions.. in our respective fields damn! One thing about this our jobs .. one case... one transaction ... one meeting .. can change your Life all round.

A sexy lady enters the office with a document ... goes to **Hassan T esq**

Lady – this is the photocopy sir

Prosecutor Hassan T – give that to the Manager .. (faces Manager) that's your statement to the Police .. make sure you study it overnight .. what you will say tomorrow must correlate to that piece of paper you are holding (lady leaves office after giving the Manager the document)

(Manager and DPO notices Hassan T esq hasn't still picked his envelope on the table)

Prosecutor Hassan T – (looks at Manager ... looks at DPO... they both looked back at him.. he slowly picks up his money... opens his drawers... a silver revolver pistol with a pack to bullets by the side is seen.. he neatly puts the envelope in the drawer.... Smiles) don't worry I'm not reporting anybody this time

(in Prison)

Tunde... Barrister and Susan on set

Barrister – well... this brings up to the end of your interview today.. we shall watch how things unfold in court tomorrow .. but I assure you.. we will try our best (Stands up and prepares to leave)

Susan – uhmm.... Sir .. I think I have a few questions I want to ask

(Barrister looks at Tunde... both of them looks at Susan)

Susan – (voice shakes a bit) you ... uhm .... You said you called the DPO first on that day?

Tunde – Yes ?

Susan- (more confident) that means you know DPO prior to the incident?

Tunde – Yes

Susan – How?

Tunde – I've known him since he was an inspector about 10 – 12 years ago.. I cant really remember ... he was part of the team that helped me investigate the gang of thieves that murdered my parents in cold blood

Susan – that must be really devastating

Tunde – hmmm ... tell me about it

Susan – did the team ever uncover the people that perpetrated the act?

Tunde – they didn't .. they kept on telling me investigation was ongoing till I got tired of calling them .. until I called the DPO recently

Susan – which landed you in prison?

Tunde – (looks down.. shakes his head) yes..

Susan – what type of duress did they put you before making that statement?

Tunde – (zones out)

Flashback

Sergeant Steven – Mr. Tunde .. I know its too early for to just spill the truth.. but I will really like if you make it easy for me.. rather .. for the both of us.. please.... And please make it easy (pauses a bit) for us .... where is ur gang? Or... where are the others? The people that robbed the bank?

Tunde –I've told you before ... I don't know...

Steven – (gives him his palms)... hanhan han han han... I don't have this time.. u see.. im an ibo boy ... as much as I like my job.. what I do... im only interested in the business aspect.. u know .. the money part ... I don't torture people to tell me the truth ... the only thing I can do.. is mediate .. a gentleman's approach.. which is what im doing right now... so I'm going to ask you for the last time.. where is your gang?

Tunde – sir.. I dont... (steven interjects)

Steven – I...i.. what? Ooh .. you don't know them? (pats him on his shoulder) im going to be leaving you in good hands .. meet Kamoru..(he was just by his side).. uhhmm.. I will also advice you to contact your lawyer .. that's if you have one.. before tomorrow

...Uhmmm... Mr. Tunde .. Unlike me .. Kamoru is an Hausa boy.. he doesn't really like business part.. he likes the action... but the DPO and I .. we support him.. every once in a while.. kid's passionate about his job...

(different flashbacks is seen of how Kamoru tortures different suspects.. . showing different skills and funny tools he has used to deal with people in the past as Steven continued Kamoru introduction)

Steven - He has unorthodox ways of eliciting evidence from my witnesses... as in .. I bank on him anytime.. he has 86% success rate.. the remaining 16% are the people that died as a result... but then... they were guilty anyways.. because they always confess... (raises voice a bit)

Tunde - Please don't do this..

Steven - Its late ..im handing you over (stands up and leaves the room... Kamoru starts talking to Tunde)

Kamoru - Its already late .. its 8'O clock pm .. I pur don close since 6pm .. I want go house.. my uncle dey house .. I wan see me before he come comot.... tomorrow morning (smiles) we start your case

Next day (the wall clock at the Counter of the Police station tells 5am)

Tunde was brought out of his cell .. takes him to a door with inscription "INTERROGATION ROOM"

Tunde was tied down .. well tied on a normal chair .. plus a rope to his neck tying him firmly to the back of the chair .. hands tied firmly to the handle of the chair.

Kamoru brings out briefcase.. Suspense ... as Kamoru unlocks the briefcase.. he didn't open it ..   he notices bloodstain at the side facing Tunde .. he calls for tissue paper from his assistant .. he collects the tissue paper and cleans the bloodstain.. throws tissue in the dustbin

He opens the briefcase .. a brand new white and blue bathroom slippers is seen

He slowly brings it out... starts talking

Kamoru – on a normal day.. I don't do exercise .. you see this room? This na my gym.. you see this slippers? I will count 6000 slaps on your face.

Kamoru - are you ready to confess?

Tunde – confess what? I've told you (Kamoru interjects...)

Kamoru – Sssshhhhh! ... first of all... I want you to Shepe for yourself...(means "curse yourself")

Tunde – Shepe ?

Kamoru- yes ...Shepe before we start... u know ... just like National anthem in any national ceremony .. oya oya...

Tunde – (sings Davido's song) okay... "shawtie want a Million dollars.. Shepe!"

(Kamoru turns to his assistant .. smiles and sings together)

ALL – say make I waya waya (Tunde's stops singing..)

Kamoru – Nooo .. continue... (as Tunde Continues... Kamoru dances towards Tunde and lands him slippers slap like 12 times rapidly with Kamoru's assistant counting)

(pauses after 12 slaps)

Kamoru- Where is your gang ? where is your gang?

Tunde – please I don't know anything...

(Scene .....fades off... focuses back on Kamoru's assistant)

Kamoru's Assistant – 243, 244, 245.. (camera shows Kamoru sweating profusely and he was already tired .. but he kept on slapping Tunde) 250, 251...

Tunde – (battered face) I will talk .. I will talk...I ... am.. part of the robbers"

Kamoru – You go talk??

Tunde – Yes yes

Flashback ends

In Prison

Susan – you were there when your parents were murdered?

Tunde – Yes

Susan – I can only imagine...

Another Flashback'

(Tunde was 12 years old)

(Hard knocks on the door about 8 times sometime in the a.m)

Gang Leader – (shouting...) Open this door ... else we will break it down .. we don't have time to waste! Open this door!

Tunde's Father – (terrified) ha ...Who.. who is that? Ok ok ... we know who you are but.. the.. the person you looking for does not live here.. neither do we have what you want .. ehn?... please its late ... come back tomorrow..

Gang Leader - what?? If we open this door ourselves.. we will kill everybody .. we won't even hesitate...

Tunde's Father - ha... ok ... Ok (opens door... three men and a chubby boy enters armed to the teeth)

Gang Leader – what? Are you even serious? We should come back tomorrow?

Tunde's Father – I'm sorry sir...I'm so sorry... seemed like the right thing to say.. I'm sorry.

Gang Leader – ok............. ok .. no wahala .. see we didn't come here for troubles neither .. I came for the money u withdrew at the bank about 2pm the One hundred Thousand Naira ...u see .. we've been unto you for a while now .. and we have our sources.. if you don't bring it out... we will take turns and rape this your beautiful wife right in front of you and your baby boy right here... so for the last time.. where is the money?

Tunde's Father – me? 2pm.. ha.. I didn't withdraw any money ... pleass...

Gang Leader – its ok... Hadji (holding a club) ... Skolla *"boy with the vespa bike"* (Holding a machete) search this house ...Most Belli cover me (Most Belli is a chubby Twelve years old with a protruding Belli holding a revolver pistol)

Gang Leader is seen holding a semi-automatic Pistol – was about to assault Tunde's mum.. while struggling.. his gun went off.. killing Tunde's mum instantly... gun dropping on the floor .. the gang leader was shocked... he was as high as kite... on dry gin.. his breadth was oozing in the whole house ..... silence ....dead silence ... blurry slow motions showing everyone's surprise faces ... gunshot sound attracts Skolly and Hadji who at that time, had found the money... rushes back to the living room.. young Tunde hiding his head)

Tunde's Father - You killed my wife! Haaa.. Bolaji.. bolaji .. see ehn .. you wont be alive to nurse your kids... O .. yeeee! (Crying loosing control)

Gang Leader – will you shut up? you want me to put a bullet in your head? Ehn.. if she didn't struggle.. would she have died? .. I'm sorry for the unusual turn of events.. (interjects)

Skolla – found it .. hahan.. Oga wetin happen? (comes in with a bag... gives his boss)

Gang Leader – (rushes to confirm the money forgetting to pick his gun from the floor) .. I didn't shoot her o .. na accident (as he opens bag and brushes through the money feeling accomplished)

Moments of Tension

Young Tunde – (on the floor scared for his life .. sobbing)

Tunde's Father – (Picks up gang leader's gun.. points at him)

Gang Leader – (raises his hands up dropping the bag of money on the table)

Bang!!'

Tunde's Father – (TF drops on the ground .. gasping and spitting blood... gasping)

Most Belli shot him!

Gang Leader – (picks his gun up points at Tunde) young blood .. I'm in a good mood today.. I'm gonna spare you.. in future.. (pointing finger at Tunde) always tell the truth .. don't lie..

(they leave the house with money)

Flashback ends..

In Prison

Susan – Its surprising your parents died from armed robbers ... and more surprising, coincidental that you are facing life sentence or even death all emanating from a robbery .. hmm.. I'm starting to think it's a generational thing... you know ?? (looks at Barrister)

(Tunde zones out seems to remember another thing)

...continuation of previous flashback

(peeps leaves the house with money)

Young Tunde – ... (crying with tears) Mummy ... Daddy wake up!!

Tunde's Father –(dying slowly) easy .. arrrgghhh easy (in pain) hmm.. Tunde ... bullet is painful... arrggghhh...

Young Tunde – sorry Daddy sorry... let me call ... our neighbor we can take you to the hospital..

Tunde's Father – Come.. come.. its late... don't worry .. let me tell you something Olatunde Ajisafe.. that Is your name ... in your life .. don't respect money... when you make it .. you spend it .. but have some savings.. make sure you live life to th... arggh... arrrggghhh...

Young Tunde – ok sir.. please don't die.. don't leave me alone..

Tunde's Father – Ajisafe is your name .. it means we are happy people .. it is in our family culture to spend and also to make others happy..(speaks very weakly and slowly) if you don't, it has its nemesis .... don't forget this ...(dies)

Young Tunde – No Sir I won.......nt (voice shakes) forget Sir.. (Bursts into more tears) Daddy ... daddy *!!*

flashback returns

In Prison

Susan – huh? Did they ever apprehend them?

Tunde starts crying

Tunde stands up to leave ... leaving barrister and Susan on sit

Tunde – we will see tomorrow in Court ... this is too much (closes the door behind him)

Barrister – (faces Susan) what have you done?? (ask gently)

Susan – these are harmless questions sir... I wonder why he is crying

Barrister – ok... lets go

Trial day

"silence Court In Session"

Reporter in front of a Camera

Reporter – today is the first day the prosecution will call their first witness in Tunde Ajisafe's case ... a question comes to mind... Is Mr Tunde Ajisafe guilty of the bank robbery? Or most importantly for the murder of the 4 policemen? Stay tuned as we continue to give you updates as the trial continues...

inside the Court

Tunde was brought in with shackles with two prison wardens behind him... this is the calmest he's been.. he quietly goes to sit behind with his escorts... calmly.. the Court hasn't started sitting yet... Tunde looks around for his wife, she's no where to be found

His work Manager walks inside the Court wearing a suit ...this is the first time his is putting on a suit.... he looks whether Tunde has been brought from the Prison.. he sees Tunde... smiles... goes to meet him

Work Manager – Mr. Tunde ... how have you been?

Tunde – Thanks ...for the support ... uhhm.. I've been fine .. I'm okay

Work Manager – to be honest... personally I've missed you .. at work... I always love your points of criticisms ... you know ... you were always constructive .. (sad face)

Tunde – (smiles) don't worry .. all this wont last .. in a moment .. I will be out, I will be back soon

Work Manager – (looks down.... Disappointed) ... yes... about that... I mean... I hate to do this ... but management made a decision .. you know... you are on news and everything ... ...well ... I was asked to ... to..... (puts hand inside the inner breast pocket of the suit... brings out a brown envelope... "Tunde's sack letter" ... Tunde collects and opened the letter... he had a straight face throughout)

Tunde – (talk to himself with a blank face............ slowly) don't worry Tunde.. you are not dead yet ... you will be fine

3 hard knocks on the door which signifies the beginning of Court session

Judge walks in with his regalia ... heads for his sit ... everyone sits ...

Outside the Court

Jess was seen cat-walking in a black and wine color corporate wear... about to enter the Court ... she got to the entrance ... peeps inside the court to see if the court is sitting ... the court is sitting ... so she backs up a bit to touch up

After touching up in front of her small mirror ... she removes the mirror and bends to put the mirror inside her handbag .... She looks up... She sees Ireti, Tunde's wife

Jess – Jesus! (shocked)

Ireti – that's right.. Jesus! And at the mention of that name.. every knee shall bow and all tongues confess that .. he is my Lord and savior ... Jessica, you are not welcomed here .. you are a bad energy.. My husband told me everything ... and I've forgiven him (points finger)... if you still refuse to back off from him... I will prove to you that Jesus still sits on the throne ... do you understand me? (raised her voice...)

Police at the entrance – hey.. keep it low, court is sitting

Jess – Ok ... (afraid) ok ... no problem Ma (takes her leave)

Tunde's wife enters the Court, sits down at the extreme right... in front ... close to the dock... close to Tunde in the accused box

Tunde sees her ... She smiles at Tunde ... Tunde faked a smile ... faces the Judge

Prosecutor (Hassan T esq) – My Lord, we are ready for trial ... however our first witness just called me, that he has a flat tyre... that he has already put in his spare and he is close to the Court he will join us soon, ten minutes tops.. he will be here (Susan interjects...)

Susan- My Lord, the business of the day is for the Prosecution to call their witness.. if they are not ready .. my Lord should strike out the matter for want of diligent prosecution

Judge – (smiles) Miss Susan .. you must be new at the Bar?

Susan – that's correct my Lord

Judge – well... that application is premature for now ... case stood down for ten minutes

Prosecutor (Hassan T esq) – My Lord .. I'm surprised the defence counsel is being too forward... but then... we will encourage the young ones air their thoughts... (laughs) I will let the sleeping dog lie ... on a lighter note my Lord ... the Attorney General of the state Sir Alphonsus is here to witness this proceedings

(Mr. Alphonsus stands up... waves his hands to all)

Judge – you are welcome Mr Alphonsus

(Mr Alphonsus takes a bow)

Inside a moving Benz

Bank Manager – (inside court premises he makes a turn... makes another Turn... sees a Lady with her head inside of her car and her red skirt visible outside... it is as if she is trying to put her bag on the passenger seat from the driver's side on a standing position) wow... just look at that..

(he pulls over right beside her car.... Jessica's car)

Bank Manager – wow wow wow...

Jess – comes out of the car

Bank Manager – (turns his car off...he's wearing a shirt and suit.. no tie) Hello pretty lady

Jess – (refuses to answer... rolls her eyes... gives attitude..)

Bank Manager – Its you I'm talking to... (holding like 3 papers flimsily) come over.. here .. roll with the big boys.. do you know who I am? Im a star everywhere I go... im even a star witness in one of the Courts in this complex today .. so just know I'm a big boy

Jess – (smiles ... looks at bank Manager from head to toe... she likes the way he dressed) well... I don't just like giving my numbers out to strangers.. that's all

Bank Manager – come on .. I'm not a stranger .. hold on ... (checks his pockets.. brings out a paper and pen) write me your number ... put your account number by the side ..

let me credit you a token .. you will realize you are dealing with a man in the system.. the money system

Jess – (rolls her eye...writes out all details.. gives the Bank Manager back his pen and paper)

Bank Manager – (smiles) you will hear from me in a minute ... uhmm... let me go now ... im already late ... are you sure you don't wanna go with me or are you busy with something?

Jess – (seemed to have completely fallen for the manager.. but confused) well... not really .. im not busy... (closes her car door mistakingly...) uhm .. I'll join you shortly

Manager – okay ... let me run , I will see you inside (manager hurriedly leaves Jess at the parking lot with the papers he is holding)

Meanwhile ... Jess had mistakingly locked her car keys and her phone in the car.

Manager – (Runsback to his car with the papers) sorry dear I forgot to drop this.. I wont be needing it inside ... (puts the paper in his car... notices Jess is stranded) what's wrong dear?

Jess – don't worry about it .. I locked my keys... in the car

Bank Manager – Ohh ... sorry about that, well by the way.. did you get the alert?

Jess – No ... not at all.. my phone is in my bag which is also in the car .. so I haven't seen it

Bank Manager – my bad .. honestly .. well I transferred a hundred k to you.. just manage that .. ive got more for you later you know?

Jess- really? Thanks a lot .. thank you .. you know what? I might need to get somewhere .. i.....i don't think I can come watch your case again... we can always hangout any other time.. I will get someone to help with my.. (Bank manager's phone starts ringing)

Screen displays *"Prosecutor Hassan T esq calling.."*

Prosecutor Hassan T – where the hell are you?

Bank Manager – (whispers to Jess) I will talk to you later ... Uhmm...Sir (talking to Hassan T) ... Im already at the parking lot ... I will be in the court in less than a minute (he paces fast to the court)

(In Court)

Bank Manager in the witness box .. a bottle of water In front of him

 Prosecutor Hassan T – Tell us what you know about The Accused

Bank Manager – I mean .. he is one of the bank's customers .. he started coming to the bank more frequently since like.. the middle of last month when he made a deposit of five million ...

Prosecutor Hassan T – tell this court the reason you believe he is involved in the bank robbery on that particular day

Bank Manager – to be honest... all the armed robbers were masked ... but one of the robbers has the same body build with Mr. Tunde .. gestures like him and even walks like him...

Prosecutor Hassan T – wait a minute ... you said he walks like him?

Bank Manager – yes

 Prosecutor Hassan T – do you know him that well to know the way he walks?

Bank Manager- (with an emotional face) yes my Lord.. he comes to the bank too much .. that I start to question if he actually has a job, I didn't know.. he has an evil plan he was about to hatch ... My Lord ... Mr. Tunde once asked me.. during one of his visits of how many armed policemen we have in the bank... My Lord (sobbing) the armed Policemen are the ones killed in cold blood on that day..

Prosecutor Hassan T – that will be all for this witness in Chief

Defence Counsel Susan – My Lord, before I go into cross examination.. (Barrister is seen in the gallery wearing an orange Shirt) I want to state as my opening statement

"Justice is a three way traffic, Justice for the Accused ... which is in this case, the Defendant (gestures toward Tunde) .. justice for the State .. whose societal norms have been desecrated and Justice for the deceased, who souls are crying in the heavens... for vengeance"

(Prosecution nods his head multiple times in agreement with Susan ...... looking sideways ...)

Bank Manager in the witness box takes a sip from the bottle water in his front, cleans his sweaty face with his handkerchief.. he couldn't believe how sound the young Lady lawyer is

Susan – (continues...) Secondly, I will like to assist this Court .. in arriving at a conclusion that there are a lot of grey areas in this matter .. My Lord .. if at the end of this case , we don't have answers to those questions, the reasonable doubt will be resolved in favour of the Mr. Tunde here

Judge – (nods in agreement)

Susan - My lord im sorry if I'm talking much instead of actually cross examining the witness, this is the first time I would be afforded the opportunity to lead in a case ... (Barrister is seen in the gallery) I thank my Lord for the opportunity (smiles)

My Lord... may I start the cross examination??

(Bank manager cleans the sweat on his face again)

Judge – its you I'm waiting for

Susan – So witness...

Bank Manager – (fidgets a bit... but hides it)

Joseph's trail

Chapter Eight

The day at the court wasn't bad at all.

Susan did marvelously well

Shook the Bank Manager terribly at cross examination

The Judge even commended Susan's performance "gave an interesting ruling why Seniors should encourage Juniors to be lead Counsel while handling cases, even the serious ones"

But the Manager stuck to the script .. he didn't change an inch of his story, even under Susan's wrath

However, Susan punctured some holes in the case against Tunde

Were those holes enough to keep Tunde out of prison?

Those are thoughts on Tunde's mind

For some reasons,

He was happy.. he spoke to his wife for a period of one minute before he was taken back to prison .. with absolutely no privacy.. he didn't let the sack letter from work bother him.

He even considered having a cigarette for the first time in his Life

You remember that junkie looking prisoner that came to disturb Ireti and Tunde at the private office?

That was Tunde's connect for the celebration of a sign of hope ..

Suraj was sitting on a short fence, smoking cigarette .. watching his fellow prisoners play football (old tyres were used as goal post)

Tunde – my man how far?

Suraj – Ha... my Accountant .... How far na?

Tunde – Suraj.. I don't tell you before... im not an accountant

Suraj – ehhh? You are not Accountant... ok .. ok ... what you are? Or what you do? What are you?

Tunde – (looks sideways) im a surveyor

Suraj – Ha ... surfyor general!! (raises his hands) oya now... so what can I do you for? (in shabby british accent)

Tunde – My lawyers made me happy in Court today, so I said I should celebrate

Suraj – Haaa... odayan mo! (means "you recognize game") see im the carpon .. out here .. if you want models.. I mean .. video vixen type, I can provide it for you... im the only person that has that kinda connect... you feel me?

(Suraj does not look like someone that can do anything other than smoke cigarette and indian hemp if he has an opportunity)

Tunde – yeah.. I feel you .. well I don't need a video vixen .. I just need a stick of cigarette

Suraj – a stick of Cigi? A stick of Cigarette .. see how you talk am? Its only bosses that smoke cigarette around here .. well.... It will cost you .

Tunde – how much Suraj ?

Suraj – 200

Tunde – what? For one stick?

Suraj – (mocks Tunde) yeah.. smoking isn't for broke people .. and inside here its more expensive.. so .. my friend... deal or no deal?

Tunde – Alright deal (he brings out money from his pocket gives to Suraj .. Suraj hands a stick to Tunde, lights it for him)

Tunde – (blows cigarette ... didn't cough... he didn't really take the smoke in)

Suraj – So my friend, what are you celebrating?

Tunde – heh... you know ... life ... and the fact that there is light at the end of the tunnel... you know this saying... where there is life .. (both of them completes it)

Suraj – there is hope ... (nods head in agreement ... points hand) you know... that's why I gbadun (means "like") my Accountant ... you are a motivational speaker .. but me I will remind you .. Do you feel motivated when the warder tells you light out in the night? Or get motivated when you get bullied by your cellmate ? Oga ... carry your motivation go front o ....This is the reality out here .... Let me give you example ... Every Saturday Morning we eat beans that is as watery as a baby having stomach upset ... how Is that for some reality check? Or Motivation ... im sure you have seen those beans or bean? If its one seed of bean is still beans right?) some people attend wedding eat better jollof rice .. we... we dey here dey chop beans (laughs) get the fuck outta here (says it casually)

Seems like Tunde remembered something

Tunde – you know what? I will surprise you all this Saturday .. you wont have to eat beans .. its my Birthday

Suraj – Accountant general.. sorry .... surveyor General (raises his two hands) its now I know the reason you came to me.. im your plug on anything believe me ... you want to give me the contract of that day.. don't worry .. you have come to the right place ... I will make sure (Tunde interjects)

Tunde – Suraj wait wait.. calm down ... I have my personal plug .. just wait till you see on that day

Suraj – ok ok.. make sure say...

Tunde – shhhh ... keep quite.. thank you ... this meeting is over

(Next day in prison)

Warden – You have a visitor (Tunde's wife – Ireti)

Tunde – thank you for always been there...I promise you something today... as long as you continue to love me .. I wont let you fall.. I promise you .. the love of my life, I wont let you down.. again

Ireti – don't worry about that.. we are family right ? for better or for worse ? remember? (fake smile)

Tunde – yes I remember (brings out cheque book from his pocket...) can I use your pen?

Ireti – (hands him a pen... Tunde writes cheque gives to his wife)

Tunde – that's a cheque of five hundred thousand Naira.. you remember Saturday is my birthday? I want you to buy a cow ... I have made arrangement with the people here ... we are going to slaughter the cow here ... and cook the food here, the caterers are going to help with that...you don't need to join in doing anything ... just buy everything you think I will need...

Ireti – (nods her head)

(scene fades out)

Same Night in prison

Warden – everybody Lights out ... lights out!! (uses his club to make annoying sounds on cell gates)

(Tunde is seen in his cell switching the lights off... his cellmate is already sleeping)

He rolls a piece of clothing and makes it into his pillow

He picks up a book titled "How to be a Lawyer in this country" and starts reading with a small rechargeable lamp by his bedside

(Warden shouting "lights out" is heard echoing and fading away from a long distance)

He lays down on his bed and within a few minutes .. he fell asleep with the book dropping to the ground

(shabby images that represents dreaming)

Tunde is seen in a very thick forest at night

The ambience was pitch black

He couldn't see anything

He puts his hand in the pocket and brings out a match stick .. the last match stick in the box. He used it to light a stick .. the stick becomes his lantern.

He could use it to see through the forest

As he was going .. finding his way

He came across a black tree .. with black leaves but one glowing fruit

Just one

You could tell because it's the only thing on the black tree glowing

Tunde looked at it closely

Moved closer and puts his lantern about a meter away from the tree

He picks up a little stick and threw it at the fruit..

He missed .. the stick hangs to the tree

Nothing on the ground again for Tunde to pluck the fruit with

The only stick is stuck on the tree.

Suddenly

A dark little boy wearing dark brown elephants grass round his waist

Runs across and carried Tunde's lantern .. almost disappearing into the woods

Tunde chases him, unafraid

Collect's his lantern back

The boy turns back, laughs .. and disappears

Tunde goes back drops the lantern

Thinks about climbing the tree

A dark young man appeared also with brown elephant's grass around his waist

With a skull of a human being round his neck as necklace

He must have been a fashionable person when he was human

Or maybe he likes treasures

He appeared beside Tunde's Lantern

Picks it up and puts out the light

Shreds the stick on the ground

He's different, He came to fight

The both started fighting

Tunde was furious

His adversary was more angry

Tunde was able to carry him up from the ground

Returns him with high gravitational speed

His back to the ground

defeated

Tunde became angry

Cuts of the skull on his chest

Threw the skull towards the fruit

He caught it once this time, hitting the target

He realized

He didn't even need the lantern

The fruit was glowing

The fruit landed straight on his hand

As he caught it

His father's spirit appeared

Calls his name in local dialect

Tunde omo Ajisafe! (Ajisafe in Yoruba literally means "wake up to jolly")

The spirit of his father and the fruit turn to light white smoke and fizzled away

The whole screen dissolves

(increasing sound echoes is heard from afar)

Warden – wake up … wake up!! (making annoying sounds on Cell gates to wake prisoners up)

Tunde wakes up in the cell … picks up the book he was reading from the floor his cellmate was already wearing his sandals

Edibles

Chapter Nine

I mean .. what could Ireti purchase with the five hundred thousand Tunde gave her for his birthday? Tunde already told her to buy a cow, the prison Tunde is has 152 inmates

Even though it's a maximum correctional facility, It is not the headquarters

So Ireti's target is at least 200 guests, She put the wardens in her estimate

She got the Cow which took the chunk of the money and many other things that makes a party rosy.

She decided to let it go

To let it go because of the good times

To let it go because of Daisy

To let it go because forgiveness is part of the bargain

She carries herself with prestige anywhere she goes

People at her workplace will call her

"the wife of that armed robber"

It didn't let it that get to her

She works even harder to keep her mind off things

That she became the most productive staff at the office

So she bought cabbage incase the wardens permits the prisoners to grill

She got Onions and every other ingredients that will land Jollof or fried rice

She hired 5 external caterers to help the prison cooks to deliver her mandate

Tunde already told her she shouldn't join them in cooking

She agreed she wont touch a piece

But manned the position of a supervisor

Tunde hasn't been too free with money

That's why he doesn't know his wife understands the art

The art of spending

He ordered two cakes 2 days ago

One of the cake says "Happy Birthday hubby"

The pink one says "happy birthday daddy.. mummy says I can't come"

Today is the day.

The Chief prison warder is seen in his office anxiously looking at his cctv camera on screen... looks at his watch .. looks back at the screen

He sees a big pick up vehicle approaching

Chief Warden – (picks up intercom) yes.. yes Open the gate, its them

The gate was wide open before the truck got close, The vehicle entered and Tunde's wife was sitted right beside the driver

They drove to the back

A live Cow to was there too

How they manage to put him at the back of the truck, with a shitload of goodies I don't know. She even bought a live goat with her own money for the barbeque that will serve as deserts

The Chief warden anticipates their knock on his office door

So swiftly he sits on his chair and turn backwards

Knock knock!

Chief Warden – come in .. you're welcome (still turning his back with both hands locked together)

One warden opens the door for Tunde's wife and one other caterer, both carrying the cakes, They Put the cakes on Chief warden officer's table

Chief warden turns back to face them..... slowly.. he sees the cake

Chief Warden – why do you think I am going to permit this? Do you know I can confiscate all these things you have bought? I will just tell the government we don't trust the source .. that's if they get to know... that it may be an attempt to poison us .. we don't need your food, we ...we (stammers) we have enough food here.. (licking his lips as he's regularly distracted by the icing on the cake)

Ireti – (smiles.. brings out an envelope from her bag slides it on the table slowly toward chief warden)

Chief Warden – (collects it fast and puts it in his drawers) err mm ... you can go and start .. what's delaying you? Mehnn... "err mm .. where's that boy sef"?

(In Tunde's cell)

His cell gate is wide open

The song "Happy birthday to you ... starts playing in the background"

He stands up from his bed with style .. wears his slippers with style

His bed is exquisitely decorated with colours of his book and had decorated his bedsheets with colourful flowers

He started dancing in a funny way

Steps out of his cell with one of his legs showing first

Dancing in a blue prison uniform looks funny

But he danced away anyway

Slow motions of how he is shaking other inmates through their cellgates

Like a celebrity

Prison wardens passing by in slow motion saluting Tunde with *swagger*

Still in slow motion

He made his way to the Chief warden's office

Song fades off as he

Knocks the door

His wife hugs him as he enters (Happy Birthday song continues..)

Chief wardens clapping his hands for them

With Cuban cigar in his mouth

All still in slow motion

The caterer seen smiling

(Song ends)

Ireti – One more thing sir? I bought this shirt for him, that's his birthday gift

Chief warden – hmm.. how thoughtful, let me see

Ireti – (brings out the shirt .. still well packed in its packet ... she gives it to chief warden)

Chief warden – looks at it .. ha hannn ... this is my size? I mean ... I will confiscate this one (attempts to put it in his drawers)

Ireti – Please sir ..dont confiscate it, I .. I just want to see him in it today after today you can collect it .. I .. I know its not allowed

Chief warden – Don't forget to give me back this evening ... you understand? (pointing at Tunde)

Tunde – Ok sir

Merrymen

Prisoners are seen at different places in total merriments

The atmosphere is filled with happiness

Some are seen with that cone clowns put on children's heads at circus

With inscription

Happy Birthday

Some fat and bulky prisoners are seen grilling the goat meat

I forgot to mention

They killed that cow

None of the cooks is experienced on how to kill a cow or skin it

Especially a big one like this

So it took up to ten prisoners to subdue the animal

Since they killed it,

They decided to do everything concerning the animal

The burning

Washing

Cutting

Separating bones from the meat was the tedious part

But they did it

They had nothing else doing

No chores for them today

It was Tunde's birthday

It is was like a public Holiday for them in the prison

That junkie prisoner (Suraj) Tunde broke the news of the party to first

gave the day a name.

(Suraj is seen with Tunde and 6 others ... Tunde is looking different in a Blue ralph lauren corporate shirt but in his prison shorts and slippers... a bottle of Jack Daniels is on the floor, all holding red cups)

Suraj – Prison's Tunde's day .. from now henceforth ... today is declared a public holiday. Even next year we are going to celebrate in style (Tunde looks at him funny .. all burst into laughter... Suraj pick up the bottle of whiskey and pours some for himself.....takes a sip... an inmates serving small chops gave him a plate.. he feels happy about the way he was served with the small chops ... he prays for the inmate in Yoruba) wo .. oma a da fun e (meaning it will be better for you.. the one serving smiles and goes away)

I cannot overemphasized all the things Ireti brought for the party

But she delivered

It was an herculean task

Still she delivered

Without any recourse to the issue on ground

She already told herself that since that incident of her and Jess at the Court the other day, she won't bring the matter up again.

All the 205 people present in prison that day at least got something

From fruits to either jollof or fried rice with a big piece of our cow friend, small chops and barbeque as deserts

Juice and liquor.. with Can beers enough to go round

Rumour has it that even prison wardens took raw meat home to their respective families

The Chief warden confiscated the remaining 2 cartons of beer.

Cigarettes and tooth picks were even shared in the evening around 4:45pm when the barbeque was ready

Ireti during the merry managed to be in the background once or twice (smiling at the mood)

Only one prisoner did not eat that day

When asked, he said he was not aware

The story of the guy is that, he always hides himself away every Saturday

So as to avoid work

His contention was Saturday is weekend, they are not supposed to work on Saturdays

So he's the only person that takes 2 days off in a week in the prison

There was no music at the birthday, it could had alerted him

So since around eleven a.m when they started preparing the food till six pm the party was called off.. he was hiding

He asked Tunde why he didn't tell him

Tunde said he wanted it to be a surprise
only Suraj knew because he felt the need to throw a party
When he shared a smoke with him,
Something about celebrating little wins

But that one prisoner got something
A pack of toothpick
The one Tunde kept for himself
Poor guy
He took one for the team

Tunde had changed back to his prison cloth
His shirt has been seized.

It stands

Chapter Ten

So it happened the Bank Manager and Jess have been having an affair low key

But Jess doesn't know that it was in Tunde's case the Manager was a witness

Incidentally, the Manager still met her at her car at the court's parking lot

Jessica's reason was that she locked her phone in the car,

That no mechanic or any one of such is around the court premises

She was hoping to see someone who could open the lock from outside

She had managed to force one of the window down but not enough room for her hand to pass

When the Bank Manager came back, he was surprised to still see her there

She has been on the same spot for at least 45 minutes, clueless

Well.. the Manager was able to get a cloth hanger from one of the security men around, he straightened it and opened the door for Jess, it wasn't easy but he did it

Jess was turned on, They got laid that same afternoon at a five star hotel around the corner

This chapter is not for any of this two

Its for Tunde and with maybe one of them or both

(In Prison)

Warden – You have a visitor

(Tunde, Barrister and Susan in a Private office)

Tunde – Barrister ... you came late o, you know they wont allow anyone enter again from 6... its already 5:30pm, you mean my case is no longer serious? Have you forgotten how much I paid you?

Barrister – lets go straight to the reason we are here .. if it was your case I wouldn't have come anyway .. I'm no longer appearing, you know...?

Tunde – yes.. its because you didn't appeal.. if as the judge gave his ruling keeping you from appearing in my case, you appealed immediately .. you will still be my lawyer in court ... there is this book I've been reading "how to be a lawyer in this country" its from there I know its your fault im not on bail .. its from there I know you coulda still been my lawyer in court .. its because you didn't appeal... see .. lets forget that... maybe when im done with the book I will borrow you.. so you wont make that mistake again .. ehn.. (nodding his head) you will learn from it

Barrister – (looks at Tunde with disbelief for a while ... he raises his voice suddenly) you were the one who bribed a federal prosecutor right inside the court without consulting me first!

Tunde – well... let us all calm our nerves... (looks at Susan)

Tunde – I'm sorry .. Barrister Susan .. how are you ?

Susan – Im fine sir ...

Tunde – you did well the other day .. I hope you do better tomorrow... see when you people get me out of here.. I will appreciate you personally (pointing finger to Susan) .. I already paid your Senior nothing concerns him then .. so Susan, make me proud tomorrow

Barrister – She won't have to do much tomorrow.. you might walk Free tomorrow

Tunde – what do you mean she won't do much tomorrow?

Barrister – we discovered a new piece of evidence but that is not the main catch

Tunde – (surprised.. folding his hands) what is the main catch?

Barrister - the Police have caught the four armed robbers and the bank Manager... (laughs ... looks at Susan) ... that's a catch literally

Barrister – the other catch is... this little evidence we discovered, is enough to convict these new set of suspects.

(The evidence)

Barrister – you know Timothy ?

Tunde – yes .. I was instrumental to his working at the bank as an intern?

Barrister – intern ? maybe you don't know .. he is a staff now

Tunde – he has not done NYSC .. how will he be a staff?

Barrister – as if you don't know your country...well Tim came to my office on Friday ... so he played a video for me

Flashback

Tim is seen in the bank running to the Toilet

All lavatories are occupied, he was in discomfort

He was knocking the three toilet doors at random at a particular interval

The people using the toilets refused to open their respective doors

Tim danced around a bit .. in discomfort

Remembers the Bank manager is not in the office yet and he's the custodian of Manager's key

He goes to his drawers ... picks the Manager's office keys, he Opens Manager's office

He rushes to his toilet, removes his trousers

The belt posed a little threat

But he was able to empty his bowel neatly

He was quite in time

After he has relaxed for some minutes

He looks around the Toilet

He sees a saucer with a half smoked weed

And a lighter

He recognizes it because his roommate in school smokes indian hemp

It wasn't his business

So he brings out his phone

Opens the camera application

He starts recording himself taking a dump

Just his face ofcourse .. not the dump

I'm sure he is not the only person that does that

He suddenly hears the horn from the car of the Bank Manager

He peeped from the toilet window

He saw the Manager driving inside the compound

The manager's office is upstairs, so it was easy for Tim to see his car

Tim quickly rushed... used tissues to clean himself up, flushes the toilet

Disinfects his hands and rushed out of the Manager's Office... keeping the door behind him under lock and keys

The Manager shouldn't know he was ever in his office.

Bank Manager – (Rushes inside the bank ... wearing a native attire...holding his suitcase .. he rushed to Tim's desk.. trying to comport) where is my key?! where is my key ?!! where is my office key?!!! (he said it so fast that Tim said...)

Tim – Huh ?

Bank Manager – my keys!! Are you deaf?

Tim – Ok .. ok sir (opens his drawers and hands the Manager his keys)

Manager rushed to his office forgetting his suitcase on Tim's table

The manager closed his office door behind him with keys

He opens back the door and rushed back to pick his suitcase up from Tim's desk,

(In Bank Manager's office)

He Drops the suitcase on his table in his office, locked the door with keys, Enters his office toilet

Tries to untangle his trousers rope.. poses a little threat

Untangles it

He's been purging from the soup he had yesterday

So He starts doing his business

Defecating

He was pressed too … that explains the reason he was rushing

He picks up his saucer … he was about to roll himself a blunt

A call comes in on his phone

Tunde Calling

Bank Manager – Ah.. Mr Tunde… how do you do today?

Tunde – im tight.. business is moving just as fine

Bank Manager – im sure you are calling back because you saw my missed call?

Tunde – Yes … as a matter of fact

Bank Manager –I just want to thank you for this boy … Tim.. no no no no … that boy is electric .. that boy na wizard o … he just repaired my Laptop that my ICT guys have been collecting money from me for …. he didn't even buy any hardware or hard disk or anything like that… ha thank you

Tunde – well.. Thank God .. im glad you guys can work together … yess .. you know.. maybe we can hangout tomorrow evening .. you know after work .. bills on me (Jess turns to Tunde in disbelief)

Bank Manager – oh how nice… great idea .. oh wait .. whats tomorrow?

Tunde – Thursday .. we can do after work.. or?

Bank Manager – im not really sure though.. I will call you tomorrow evening, I will tell Tim too.. I don't even know if the boy can hang out till late .. i no wan spoil that innocent boy

Tunde – Na malt he go drink now (both laughs) oya now

Bank Manager – Cheers

Tunde – till tomorrow (drops phone)

Still in Bank Manager's toilet (he tries to roll…)

Another call comes in

+2348 blurry numbers ending with 60 *calling* displays on screen

Bank Manager – Yes ?

Most belli – yh yh.. na we .. its us

Bank Manager – oh … what? (wants to shout initially but speaks on a low tone.. he was audible .. he was in his toilet, he had a level of privacy)

Bank Manager -   have I not told you not to call me ? … I will call you

Most belli – See we don't have time .. we need to do this thing as soon as possible, I told you before those guns don't belong to us .. we borrowed them from the Police, everyday we pay a hundred thousand.. so we need to do this thing before the week runs out

Bank Manager – see.. I want you to come for the job on Saturday when business is not usual .. I don't want innocent people to die .. if you can disarm the four policemen .. you can easily gain entrance into the bank. I will tell you when Moses will come and put money in the atm .. you will come about the same time .. If you can do this neatly without killing anyone ... I will be happy

Most belli – Ok .. Saturday right? That's your own offer .. expect us to come between now and Saturday .. once I feel it in my spirit is the right time .. you will receive us .. we must return those guns by Saturday, I don't break my promises .. I already told them we will return the tools by Saturday...

Bank Manager – Ha.. (recipient interjects)

Most belli – don't worry .. why are you scared? You are not doing anything .. are you carrying the guns with us? So why are you scared

Bank Manager – ok ok .. please don't kill anyb... (line cuts)

Bank Manager – hello hello ... (talks to himself) hmm.. today's Wednesday and they want to come on or before Saturday .. hmm god will see us through (he lights the half smoked weed)

Flashback ends

In Prison

Barrister – It was that phone that Tim forgot in Bank Manager's office that had records of the conversation... so we took it and meet Steven ... yesterday Saturday .. I heard you had a party.. (smiles) hope it was nice? sorry I missed it I was working on your case.. I couldn't come.. so back to what I was saying .. you remember Inspector Steven? Your IPO...

Tunde – yeah ... yeah... I remember (excited)

Barrister – .. its surprising he's the only one not compromised ...so we went and arrested The Bank Manager first, we used the date and time of the record on Tim's toilet video to trace the number that called the Manager at that time. We traced that number straight to a five star hotel the robbers used as hideout. They were all arrested at different rooms with 2 of their other friends hanging out with them at the time

Tunde – wow .. God is great

Barrister – I'm not done yet Mr. Tunde ... did I mention...

Tunde – mention what?

Barrister – they also arrested the DPO

Tunde – haha... (surprised) the DPO? Why?

Barrister – one of the robbers who happened to be a lady, confessed the DPO has been the one supplying them with arms. All of them are in custody now as we speak .. the Governor is aware of the new developments in the case.. and you know he has zero tolerance for these kind of things

Tunde – (shakes his head .. he was happy.. speechless)

Barrister – its 6:30 we need to take our leave ... (Barrister and Susan stand up)

Barrister – don't forget to bring a cheque of my five hundred thousand naira to court tomorrow

Tunde – Haba.. but we didn't even go into the main.. (Barrister interjects)

Barrister – don't even start.. we had a deal , besides I have delivered.. I expect you to be happy .. not to argue my fees with me .. time is far spent

Tunde – (laughs) I'm just playing with you Barrister ... you will get your balance

Susan – congratulations once again Mr. Tunde

Tunde – (smiles at her .. he was soo elated but he couldn't show it)

Susan – take care... see you in court Tomorrow

Tunde – Yes goodnight

Barrister – Goodnight (takes their leave)

One night has never been longer for Tunde

He anticipates how the proceedings will eventually go in his favour

He looked forward to how Susan will start and end her speech

Also to how the judge will finally tell him he's free to go home

His wife will be knowing for the first time in court tomorrow morning of all the new discoveries

She would have expected the trial to continue

Tunde looked forward to many things

He looked forward to what he will tell the DPO when he knew the robbers all along when they see

He didn't know what to think of the Bank Manager

But he looked forward to seeing him in his position

in the Prison

These are the thoughts ravaging his mind when his attention was caught by...

Warden – Lights out ... lights out!! (making annoying sounds with his club with cell gates)

Tunde turns over on his bed to sleep... he couldn't sleep

It was his last night in prison

Every hour on the countdown seems to have turned to different tortoises

Some slow, others really sloww

He looked forward to everything that will happen

Being anxious is an understatement

The next day in Prison

Warden – wake up wake up!! … (making annoying sounds with his club on cell gates)

Tunde wakes up and stretches, his cellmate on his knees praying

Another warden – hey you .. Tunde .. the Black Maria is waiting "means the vehicle commuting people having court trials today is waiting" .. are you even ready for Court?

Tunde rushes and brushes his teeth .. took his bath

As he was passing by..

His fellow inmates were hailing him, not because they knew he was free

But because his reputation has risen since his birthday

None of them except Tunde's cellmate had seen him since saturday

Some called him "chairman"

Others call him "Surveyor general .. or Chief Surveyor"

In appreciation for the celebration of his birthday with them

He has many loyalists

He enters the black maria (prison vehicle)

Fellow Commuter – Surveyor General! Hailings bro

Tunde – hailings bro

(In Court premises)

The Vehicle is seen arriving in court

The press and the normal settings in place

The Court is ready to sit

Lawyers well dressed

Prosecutor Hassan T esq is seen reading the newspaper

Susan alone in her corner ... looking confident as ever

Barrister goes to meet Tunde

Tunde hands him a cheque of five hundred Thousand Naira

Barrister puts the Cheque neatly in his diary

 Thirty minutes later ...

Court was about to start sitting

The familiar faces of the people present at the gallery include

Tunde's former workplace's Manager, Tunde's wife, Tim, Barrister, Several other unknown faces and the press

one woman walks into the Court with an interesting colour riot attire.. goes to the front, that was the Court's Registrar

Registrar – I need your attention please .. the Court will not be sitting today, My Lord has gone on an official assignment, I will implore counsel to come forward and agree on new dates for their cases... my lord is sincerely sorry for any inconvenience this may have caused...

Everybody on Tunde's side disappointed by the news

Susan moved forward with her diary

Measured it with the Prosecution's diary in a bid to get a new date for their case

Funny enough

Susan's diary was busier than the Prosecutor Hassan T's

Susan's law firm handles anything that has bearing with a Court

The Prosecutor handles only criminal cases for the state

That explains why

However,

After thorough comparison of diaries ... with Court's schedule

The closest date the court could afford the parties is in a month's time

Susan tried her best to bring the date closer especially when this matter is to be terminated by a simple notice to the court

That new evidence has been discovered which totally exculpates Mr. Tunde

All effort proved abortive

Tunde is seen sobbing on the side (Barrister was with him.. his diary is in his bag .. his bag is not with him at the moment)

Barrister – I mean .. this case is high profile .. but the good thing is … the Governor is already involved, butttt....a lot of things can happen within a month .. im afraid we just have to be hopeful.. lets keep our fingers crossed

Ireti comes to meet Tunde, gives him a bottle of lucozade

Ireti – (talked with themselves.. inaudibly... there was enough time for him to bring Ireti up to speed)

The irony is, all other Court rooms around are sitting, only the Judge in Tunde's matter is on an *official assignment*

Tunde is seen back in prison, downcasted.

on the Brightside,

among the numerous things that stands

the truth is one of them

it stands.

Chapter Eleven

Wow.. this life is a pot of hot beans

Tunde thinks

He's back in prison

He has to wait a whole month, before his lawyers will tell the court officially that a new evidence has been revealed

Before the Court can now discharge him

Well... he is still well respected in his space

So he decided to live it up

(he goes to meet Suraj, the Junkie prisoner)

Tunde – Yo.. my man .. How far?

Suraj – Accountant general!! .. (raises up his hands)

Tunde – abegi joor .. give me cigarette

Suraj - (hands him a cigarette with speed... lights it) I hear say your case no go on today.. I understand .. na normal dubz

Tunde –what do you mean by normal dubz?

Suraj – I know say you dey reason my matter ... even my case too .. the judge in my case is in india... presently, he has health issues ... now   .. because of his health complications.. here I am .. smoking cigarette with people like you (pointing finger towards Tunde)

Tunde –(puffs the cigarette's smoke perfectly) no worry yourself.. we dey here together "literally means we are In this together"

Scene fades off

Next day in prison

(In Tunde's Cell.. Tunde and his Cellmate are stretching .. exercising)

Warden – you have a visitor

It was Barrister (only Barrister came to see Tunde)

Barrister – I got a call from the Court's Registrar this morning .. he said only your matter is coming up today by one pm ... so you need to make arrangements for how they will take you to court

At this point ... No black maria (prison bus) is available to take Tunde to Court because it had already gone and they can't release him to his Lawyer to take him to court .. the problem now is ... who is going take Tunde to Court?

(In Chief Warden's private car on their way to court)

Chief Warden – you know I'm not supposed to do this?

Tunde looks at him

He didn't answer … he looked through the glass to feel the sense of freedom, he was not in shackles. The glass was wound up, but he could wind it down if he wanted… he winds down… brings his head out slightly… closes his eyes ….breathes in fresh air

He knew the smell.. that of freedom

One pm

(In Court)

Court sitting with only Barrister and Ireti's face tagged as familiar in the gallery

Susan – I am delighted to inform this Honorable court that… (explains the rest) and that's why we are bringing this application.. I am most obliged (sits down)

Prosecutor Hassan T esq – (Speechless throughout)

Judge –the Accused person Is hereby discharged … case numbered so … so.. so (suit number) …is hereby struck out for the prosecution to put their house in order and file another charge in this matter

The judge sat on this day solely because he knows the Governor is interested in the outcome of the bank robbery case and the need to let the innocent walk

The arrest of the Bank Manager, the armed robbers and the DPO heralds the headlines of the newspapers

So the public already knew Tunde is innocent

Regardless his wife was there, right beside him

every step of the way

Tunde is happy

He is going home

Everyone on Tunde's side is happy

Everyone who knew Tunde personally that saw yesterdays 7'o clock news

The reason the court didn't sit on his matter

And why Tunde might be in prison for the next one month

Even though the public is aware of his innocence

It all ended in happiness for him

(Outside the Court)

Journalists interviewing Tunde

Reporter – what do you have to say about what happened in court today?

Tunde – (in front of camera) I .. I don't have much to say, the only thing .. I will say is ... the police should try their best to conclude their investigation on the merit before charging people to court ... I made many friends in prison, that the systems inadequacy is the reason they are there stranded there

The Chief warden walks forward

Chief warden - Mr. Tunde ... here is your shirt (hands Tunde his shirt) remember to stay out of trouble .. it's a wicked world out there.. that's why I'm fulfilled every inmate is well taken care of.... under my care

Tunde – (nods In agreement and puts the Shirt on his wife hugs him)

Tunde .. now a free man

Has the sum of one million, two hundred naira left in his account, he has been really generous lately even to some Prison wardens who bring their personal problems to him

His belongings were handed to him

He tries to power his phone up

The phone battery was too flat

He goes home with his wife

He saw an envelope on the center table

The contents of the letter read they will be evicted within the next month if they don't pay rent

The rent is one million

He doesn't intend to pay that now

He needs to find his feet first, he just got back

Tunde – (he goes and charge his phone.. he needs to see his account balance.. it was his case they were reporting on Tv ... he saw the interview he gave)

The sum of 1,200,000 displays on screen as Tunde's balance

He had finished the sum of five million naira... right from prison ..

Legit.

So All along,

Jess's husband knew about the sex escapade between his wife and Tunde

He even knows his wife's current boyfriend is the Bank Manager

He feels sorry for the young man

Now that he's in police net ...

something bad always happen to Jessica's partners sooner or later

But he is unbothered

Because his hands too are not clean

He is homosexual, he's only into men

Not passing judgments at all .. I mean, this is a fiction

In any event, its between him and whosoever person's penis it is

He never came out ..

The terrain where he is .. does not accept that type of sexuality

But because of the pressure from his family, he got married to Jess

his parents are rich and he is the heir to all inheritance

his siblings being all girls

rumor has it that Jess was a renowed nympho at high school

but became a nun at the Catholic University she attended in the uk

she got back and got married, she met her husband at a friend's wedding.. also in uk,
she caught the bouquet at that wedding

though her marriage with her husband is an arranged one,

they both know each other's sexuality but promised to keep it secrets from everyone

it was an open relationship, so far they practice safe sex

Someone saw Jess in church last week

I mean

Who are we to judge?

At least she is making efforts

We just hope its descent.

Chapter Twelve

(A woman is seen in a local settings trying to give birth)

Matron – push ... just one final push...

Woman – ahhhh... Aaarrrghhhh!!!

(baby crying)

Matron – oh .. so cute.. he's a boy

(Following week)

(two women visit Most belli's mom.. they are poor too... staring at most belli sleeping peacefully on the old couch in the living room .. most belli's mom in the kitchen)

Woman 1 – chai .. such a handsome boy

Woman 2 – ehnn.. fine boy o..

Woman 1 – (envious) hmmm..... baby like this .. fine boy .. he is unlucky o , fine boy like this... born into a poor family .. his father is no where to be found.. hmm.. nawa oo

Woman 2 – (pitied face) may we not be unfortunate in this life

Woman 1 – hmmm .. Amen oo

Most belli's Mom – my association people... thanks a lot for coming .. (brings food for the women)

Woman 1 – eyah.. don't bother o ...but as you have brought this food for us, his future is bright already

Woman 2 – yes o ..(laughs hysterically) yes oo

(9 years later)

Most belli is a chubby 9 year old kid

(Most belli's school)

Teacher – So... (referring to Most Belli and 5 others around Ten a.m) you people haven't paid your school fees, Tell your parents to pay up ... or tomorrow , I will also send you home.. alright ...see you when you pay...go home for now

Most belli's house was quite a distance, he was in primary 4
He will have to trek all the way home
His mother would have sent someone to pick him
Her calculation was that the school will close around two pm
She sells roasted corn far away from his school

Most belli is sad as he was sent out ... he started strolling to his house
He walked for a while when someone also sent home from his school
Rode a vespa bike fast passed him
The one on the bike saw they were wearing the same uniform
Slammed his brakes
His name is Skolla
He offered most belli a ride
He agreed

He feels the guy is a fun guy

He was his senior in school primary 6

He nicknamed Most belli *most belli* because of obvious reasons

He is chubby and cute, like a young Sean Kingston

So they rode round the city

Most belli enjoyed his day that day

He lost focus totally in school and even discouraged his mother not to pay his fees

He started hustling fast on the streets

From selling indiam hemp

He distributes for Skolla who is the main dealer

Business wasn't moving as fast because it was highly competitive

Besides police arrests them frequently

Most belli developed absolute hatred for the police

Because of their unscrupulous ways

The corrupt system gave him more reasons to be bad

Setting a bad example for the society was his goals

So Most belli and his partner decided to step it up

They started robbing people

The first time he had to kill someone was when he was Twelve years old

That was the robbery in Tunde's Father's house

Tunde's father was his first victim

All along, Tunde never knew the person that killed his father is among the Bank
robbers... But he will soon come to the realization

Most belli gained popularity in the underworld after his first kill,

given his young age

He has no heart

Not only that he's trigger-happy,

He is good at it

Skolla was his bestfriend at the time

The same guy that introduced him to the first gang he had his first kill

It was his first robbery

Prior to that,

the leader of the gang had trained Most belli on how to use a revolver

a day before the robbery

so it wasn't hard for him to quickly pull the trigger when situation warrants

Most belli became more tactical in Armed robbery, Kidnapping, Assassinations
And delivery of classified packages, he is notorious

He once delivered in a neatly well packaged box

The bloddy left hand of one of his victims with his wrist watch still worn

To his family

because they won't pay ransom

the wrist watch is for the family to know its their dad.. for reals so Most belli to the police,

is Most wanted

the only thing the Police knows about him is that he is fat

he never exposes his face as he is always on mask

that's why the Lady Robber was surprised Tunde was not shot when Most belli met him mask off... if I wont err on the side of superstition, I would have said it was Tunde's father's spirit that kept Tunde alive that day.. why because ...

if you see Most Belli's face while in action, you have seen death.. literally

Most belli's charisma is ecstatic, I mean .. you will want to meet him on a normal day.. he's rich enough. He looks really responsible

but you will never know, the type of demon that hides underneath

he is handsome chubby and dresses well

he could approach anybody, anywhere..

the date he met the Bank Manager..

..Most belli was relaxing at the pool side of a 5 star Hotel one cool evening

He had a bottle of Johnny walker in front of him

And something to dilute it with

The Bank Manager was wondering around

He wanted to light his cigarette

He had no lighter

So he came to meet Most belli who was just drinking at the time

He came and borrowed his lighter

Most belli offered him a sit

Manager had nothing to lose

So he sat down

They started talking

Only God knew how they managed to confide in themselves

Till the extent they conspired

To rob the Manager's Bank

Tunde became aware when he was watching TV one day

That it was Most belli that killed his father

He remembers as he was watching him

It was on news with headline

"Police apprehends deadly gang"

Reporter on Tv – Most belli is the gang leader that led the team of robbers to rob the bank on the..... he is a notorious armed robber, kidnapper and assassin, he has been on the wanted list of the Police for 19 years

He realizes when flashback of memories where the name of Most Belli was ever mentioned ... to his hearing

Flashback of memories of

The chubby small boy that shot his father

The chubby guy he met one on one when he was following the Black Hyundai

Damn! So it was him all along? He wondered

But then he was happy

Most Belli is now in police custody

He will eventually get vengeance

The vengeance he deserves

For the loss of his Parents

And the wrongs he knew nothing about but suffered for

As for the Bank manager and the DPO, karma has already visited them

That's if there is anything like Karma

(In Governor's Office)

the Governor is having a meeting with like six other people, all in native attire

Man 1 – your Excellency sir, this is the list of officers due for retirement this year (gives the Governor a document)

Governor – so the Director for lands and development is also retiring? Hmm..

Man 2 – Yes sir .. infact he is supposed to have retired 5 years ago.. he is 70 but loves the service dearly .. I think he deserves to go and rest ... it's the deputy director's turn to be the Director

Governor – ehen? What did the deputy director study in school?

Man 3 – Economics

Governor – No ..no... no (shaking his head) I have someone in mind .. someone for the job

All – as your Excellency pleases (scene fades out)

(In Court)

The DPO, Bank Manager and the 4 armed robbers

All in one and same dock

It's a case between **State v Asi** a.k.a Most Belli and 5 others

Judge – Here is my Judgment, i find all the Defendants guilty of all heads of charges against them. This court hereby sentence them to death by Firing squad

May God Almighty forgive your souls

This Court will rise

Clerk - Court!

Camera shows Most belli's face. Emotionless.

He was going to retire after the bank job

He must have underestimated the saying that

He who lives by the gun, shall die by it

Tunde came to witness the proceedings

His mood was indifferent at the pronouncement of judgment

Jess is seen leaving a supermarket

She was not with her car this time

It was during the pandemic, So she has her mask on

Even with that, she was still attractive

As she steps out,

A man notices her...

The man was inside a nice car just by the parking lot

Jess walked by

Man - hello pretty lady

Jess gives him audience

(Tunde's house)

Tunde is seen in his house, His phone rings

"unknown number *calling* displays on screen"

Tunde – (picks) Hello?

Recipient – Hello... yes you are speaking with Emmanuel Quadri.. your state Governor

(Tunde jumps up from his sit)

His wife studying on her Computer on the dining table notices his excitement

Tunde – your ... your excellency Sir?

Governor – I want you to meet me at my office tomorrow, I learnt you are Quantity surveyor? Is that right?

Tunde – Yes yes I am.. I graduated in 2008

Governor – *Oh .. that's great, I want you to come with copies of your credentials to my office by ten am tomorrow, I will text you a number right after this call… that you will call when you are on your way*

Tunde – alright sir .. thank you your excellency .. I will be there

Governor – yeah …have a nice night (drops call)

Tunde – yes … you too sir… you too (too excited to know the call has been dropped)

Jess is seen in the man's vehicle, still with her mask on

Seems they clicked.

Epilogue

(one year later)

Tunde took the job

He is rich now, has his own house

He doesn't even have to bother about his finances again

The Governor is his friend

They are extremely close

The Governor finds Tunde humorous

He enjoys his philosophy

Lest I forget, Tunde wrote a cheque of Five hundred thousand, sends it to Susan by mail.. he pays his debt... which actually was a promise

Well

That was last year's gist

We are talking in the present

The day was Tunde's birthday

a Sunday

Guess who was present but not expected?

Suraj

That junkie

His friend from prison

The merriments atmosphere around Tunde's family is glittering

He said "its world's Tunde's day"

Ireti and Tunde's second child is on the way

They had an ultra scan

It is a boy

Everything is perfect

Ireti too had rapid promotions at work

She is the branch Manager now

But she is on maternity leave

She is seven Months heavy

Scene fades out

Tunde is seen with his family in a blue Toyota highlander Jeep

Daisy at the backsit holding a cotton candy

They got to a traffic light

(a boy comes from the back.. to Tunde's side)

Boy – Please I need money, I have not eaten since yesterday

Tunde looks forward not minding the boy .. he didn't even pity him

He looks at the timer on the traffic light

It is still Red reading 49, 48 , 47 in descending order

Tunde puts his hands in his pocket

Brings out a bundle of mint 200 naira notes ... as if he was going to give the whole bundle .... Counts it small.. gives up the counting

Removes one note and gives it to the boy

Ireti – (looks at him unbelievably... smiles) where is my husband? In fact (she opens her bag and brings out a thousand naira note and gave it to the same boy ... at this time the light had turned green)

Tunde looks at her wife in some type of way

Ireti – what? Its just money .. lets thank God we are able to give

(both of them bursts into laughter)

Tunde's final thoughts are, a poor man isn't only someone who doesn't have, but also someone who has but failed to live up to expectation, because he does not want to go broke. The poverty mentality.

(deleted Scene)

(Barrister is with Tim)

Barrister – Timothy .. if I may ask... why did you sell your boss out.. I mean .. you have done the right thing but ... I'm just curious

Tim – the truth is ... I myself .. I don't know ... but something in me changed the day I met Mr. Tunde .. somehow ... he inspired me .. he doesn't deserve to be in jail .. my conscience will judge me (smiles)

Barrister does not seem to understand

The end.

Printed by Books on Demand GmbH, Norderstedt / Germany